CHURCH JUNKIES

JOSH MELANCON

Church Junkies: A pastor's perspective of what true spiritual health looks like, how to get it and how to keep it
© 2019 Josh Melancon
FIRST EDITION, March 2019
All rights reserved.

No portion of this book may be reproduced, stored in a retrieval system, or transmitted in any form or by any means-electronic, mechanical, photocopy, recording or any other-except for brief quotations in printed reviews or articles, without the prior permission of the publisher. For information, address The People Company by email to inquiries@thepeoplecompany.org.

The various versions of Biblical scripture references have been used for clarity of meaning and are in no particular order:

The Berean Study Bible (BSB) The Holy Bible, Berean Study Bible, BSB Copyright ©2016, 2018 by Bible Hub Used by Permission. All Rights Reserved Worldwide.

The Voice (*Voice*) Scripture taken from The Voice™. Copyright © 2008 by Ecclesia Bible Society. Used by permission. All rights reserved.

The Expanded Bible (EXB) Scripture taken from The Expanded Bible. Copyright ©2011 by Thomas Nelson. Used by permission. All rights reserved.

New Living Translation (NLT)Scripture quotations marked NLT are taken from the Holy Bible, New Living Translation, copyright © 1996, 2004, 2015 by Tyndale

House Foundation. Used by permission of Tyndale House Publishers, Inc., Carol Stream, Illinois 60188. All rights reserved.

New International Version (NIV) THE HOLY BIBLE, NEW INTERNATIONAL VERSION®, NIV® Copyright © 1973, 1978, 1984, 2011 by Biblica, Inc.® Used by permission. All rights reserved worldwide.

New American Standard Bible (NASB) Scripture taken from the NEW AMERICAN STANDARD BIBLE®, Copyright © 1960,1962,1963,1968,1971,1972,1973,1975,1977,1995 by The Lockman Foundation. Used by permission.

King James Version (KJV)

New King James Version (NKJV) Scripture taken from the New King James Version®. Copyright © 1982 by Thomas Nelson. Used by permission. All rights reserved.

The Twenty-first Century King James Version of the Holy Bible (KJ21) Scripture quotations taken from the 21st Century King James Version®, copyright © 1994. Used by permission of Deuel Enterprises, Inc., Gary, SD 57237. All rights reserved.

Holy Bible: Easy-to-Read Version™ Taken from the HOLY BIBLE: EASY-TO-READ VERSION™ © 2006 by Bible League International and used by permission.

Scripture quotations marked ESV® are taken from The Holy Bible, English Standard Version®, copyright © 2001 by Crossway, a publishing ministry of Good News Publishers. Used by permission. All rights reserved.

Scripture quotations marked AMP are taken from the Amplified® Bible, Copyright © 2015 by The Lockman Foundation. Used by permission. www.Lockman.org

Any Internet addresses (websites, blogs etc.), phone numbers or company or product information printed in this book are offered as a resource. They are not intended in any way to be or imply an endorsement by The People Company, nor does The People Company vouch for the content of these sites and numbers for the life of this book.

This work is cataloged in the Library of Congress.
ISBN-13: 978-1-7337368-0-0

Book cover design by Stephanie Weibring
Published by: The People Company Thibodaux, Louisiana
thepeoplecompany.org

*To you.
Just because you haven't
made a sound,
doesn't mean God has not
heard you cry.*

TABLE OF CONTENTS

	Foreword	1
	Introduction	3
1	Jacked-Up Church	9
2	Church Rehab	25
3	More Than A Building	43
4	The Sin Issue	53
5	Red Pen Theology	63
6	Showing Up Is Half The Battle	73
7	It's Not All About The Feels	91
8	Expose the Lie, Catch the Thief	95
9	What's Next?	105
	Acknowledgments	118
	Notes	120

FOREWORD

I have known the author of this book all his life. Literally. I'm his dad. He was 11 months old when we all went to church for the first time. It started a journey that eternally changed all of our lives. Some 40 years later we are all still going to the same church and now Josh has become Pastor Josh.

This book was written because of a sincere desire to bring people to an experience that far exceeds just going to church. I personally saw the transformation our Lord did in Josh's heart as a young man. This book reflects his sincere perspective on what spiritually healthy people look like and what it takes to get spiritually healthy and remain there.

You will read about why some people don't attend church and why ultimately, we all should attend. Church was not invented by man. It was created from the heart of God when He planned the redemption of His most treasured creation - you.

Church works! Being a part of a church body is mandated by God to help every one of us become the people we were created to be. We all realize that Christians are flawed. We must also realize that Christ, His word, and Christianity are not.

May the words of this book minister to your heart and encourage you to move forward in your walk with the Lord.

Bishop Ronnie Melancon

INTRODUCTION

The early morning ring of an alarm clock has awakened me on Sundays for many years now. I grew up in church. I can tell you a lot of funny stories concerning church cultures, specifically Southern church culture. I love the church but at one point in my life I had some not so loving feelings about it as well.

I was only eleven months old when my parents walked into a loud, crazy church located on a winding rural back road in south Louisiana. Until that time most of my extended family either attended a "quiet" church or none. What my parents were about to experience was going to change the rest of their lives and mine as well. I'm glad my parents were able to overlook the strangeness of that back-road church's structure to see that Jesus had something amazing for them, and eventually, me. It was the beginning of a relationship with the Almighty and His bride, the church, like our family had never experienced. And, like every relationship, it has had its moments of testing.

There was never an exact moment of realization but

more a gradual understanding–born from many observations and experiences–that not everyone who appeared to be "Christian" on Sunday was living as "Christian" on the other days of the week. And though it was not a conscious decision, it was becoming painfully clear to me that I was falling into that category as well.

For the most part, people come to church because of needs. Pain is the greatest of equalizers. When a person grows up in church, as I did, one can take for granted what has always been there, the love and acceptance from the majority and most of all the grace and mercy of God. The abiding presence of God can seem a sure thing and can be mistaken for His approval. I had an idea about what He saved me for, my purpose, but it was not until I was in college that I understood what He saved me from. That revelation brought joy into my life but was very humbling as well.

Does the church dare to address the elephants hiding under its pews?

Church folks have been criticized for hypocrisy for decades. And sometimes that criticism is justified. Pastors caught in illicit affairs and their wives strung out on prescription drugs. Ministers' children doing things that not even unchurched kids would think to do. Church members as messed up as those who don't attend church. Yes, I've witnessed these things firsthand.

The Bible tells us Jesus Himself had no use for posers. Matthew 23: 25-28 puts it plainly: *"Woe to you, scribes and Pharisees, you hypocrites! You clean the outside of the cup and dish, but inside they are full of greed and self-indulgence. Blind Pharisee! First clean the inside of the cup and dish, so that the outside may become clean as well. Woe to you, scribes and Pharisees, you hypocrites! You are like whitewashed tombs, which look beautiful on the outside, but on the inside are full of dead men's bones and every impurity. In the same way, you appear to be righteous on the outside, but on the inside, you are full of hypocrisy and wickedness."* BSB

I once heard a woman say, "We all come from something." I've always loved that statement. It gives a sort of equality that I think we all long to experience. She was successful but had not forgotten what it felt like before all her accomplishments. The times when her struggle was stronger than her success. It made an impact on me.

Although I've pointed out some of the worst scenarios, it is safe to say that this is the perception of many people concerning the church. So how did the church drift to such disappointing places?

Stick with me awhile as I explore why something as great as what the Bible calls the *ecclesia*, the church, is falling so short of its potential and purpose, and what we can do to shift the drift.

Church doesn't have to represent all the disappointments some have experienced it to be. It can be part of the greatest experience of our entire lives. I want to challenge and test everything you think you know about *church*. Though this book exposes some of the flaws that need to be fixed in the church, I hope, if you have given up on church, it will also inspire you to give church another chance.

Few, if any, deny that they need or have needed some sort of help in a difficult time. Regardless of background, socioeconomic status, race, or other demographic, people are fragile. We need help. Jesus and His church are definitely the answer. However, when approached with an unhealthy mindset, church can create more confusion for us than we had before we attended.

I call this the "Church Junkie" test and the starting point is the first question. Before you can determine where you should be you must understand where you are now. Take your time. Go ahead. You can be honest with yourself, no one is listening.

- **What has been your experience with church up to this point?**
- **What does church represent for you?**
- **Do you dread church, but feel like you will be zapped from above if you don't go?**
- **Do you think you should call your pastor the moment something goes wrong in your life?**
- **Do you feel great when you are leaving church, but by some point in the week, you have lost all your momentum?**
- **Do you feel like you don't know how to have at home what you get at church?**

- **Do you wonder how the pastor gets those revelations from the same Bible you read and you get no revelations when you read it?**
- **Do you walk into church having barely survived the week hoping the ministry has a word that can help you go on?**
- **Do you lead a church, and yet look forward to the end of each Sunday?**

There may be more questions that could be asked that are common to the Church Junkie, but let me conclude with this one: **Do you want to know what it feels like to be like the church the Bible talks about, but you just don't know how?** If the answer is yes, then you are the one this book is written for.

If you are thinking about going to church next Sunday, either again or for the first time, I hope this book inspires you to not only go but to experience all the joy that was meant to come with it.

And it is not only my hope but also my prayer that you experience spiritual growth in Christ, and church becomes everything it was intended to be.

I pray you become more than a Church Junkie, that you become a Jesus Junkie instead.

"Just about everyone had a story to tell, an experience that shaped their view of church. And no one's perspective should ever be discounted."

- Josh

1
JACKED-UP CHURCH

What's the reason, the really *real* reason, you go to church? What do you think is the real reason others go to church? Going to church for the right reason brings true spiritual healing and a lasting sustainment to that first experience. However, attending church for a feel-good fix or as a purely social experience belittles the purpose of church and often results in a disillusionment that causes people to stop going altogether.

Unrealistic expectations and unmet expectations of church are often the very things that bring on the disappointment in the church experience or, even worse, a warped idea of what purpose God intended church to be for a believer. Expectations are tricky in that they are necessary for us to reach for more and better but can be harmful when they are misguided.

I am frustrated when I expect my problems to be over when someone prays over me, or when the preacher preaches the perfect message and then I go home to the crippling realization that my problems didn't go away.

Do you know what I have observed as I listen to faithful church attenders? They sometimes sound like drug addicts. An addict may feel that all he needs is his next fix and he will be better. The downside with that kind of thinking is that it provides a momentary fix for the craving but no long-term resolution for the problem. That temporary high doesn't last, and the crash leaves all the issues he was trying to escape still right there with him.

Is church supposed to be just an experience that leaves the attender momentarily jacked up?

Not according to Acts 2:42:

> *"The Believers Form a Community.*
> *All the believers devoted themselves to the apostles' teaching, and to fellowship, and to sharing in meals (including the Lord's Supper), and to prayer."* NLT

Take Responsibility

What if you and I started going to church to take responsibility for our personal walk with Jesus instead of ducking it?

What makes me think you are even remotely thinking of ducking your responsibility to your personal walk with God?

It's human nature.

> *"For I was guilty from the day I was born, a sinner from the time my mother became pregnant with me."*
>
> Psalm 51:5 Voice

We all want the easy way out.

But what if we understood that this coming Sunday (or whatever day or days we may attend church) was a step in the right direction of a lifelong journey? A marathon if you will, not a sprint.

That it is not about being the fastest but about endurance, persistence, and patience.

It is my complete belief that Jesus Christ is the answer and that His church is His representation on earth. I believe that God can fix us and will fix us; however, it will not be the quick junkie fix we have in mind.

After all, if you or I developed an addiction to something and have spent our entire lives up to this point controlled by that addiction, it will take some pain, patience, persistence, and training to teach us how to get free from it.

And how to stay free from it.

It's easy to give up in the process of getting better and being different. We are looking for that one sermon, or that preacher with the "magic" prayer hands. When what we need is to commit to the journey and understand that we won't make it alone.

The pain of getting better can sometimes convince us that getting better isn't a real option.

It feels unbearable, right?

But it is necessary. The pain that sometimes comes from the waiting while in a change process will put a more permanent growth in our lives that won't come from a temporary emotional high.

Pain Management

Opioids have become one of the more serious addiction epidemics of our time. I have had many friends who went from people with back injuries to people with drug addictions. For some, those pills create more problems than they solve.

The pain from a nagging injury can get to a place where the sufferer no longer cares what it takes as long as the relief is immediate. The doctors prescribe "as needed" pills that numb that pain. Then "as needed" becomes the master. We lose our purpose, our freedom, and yes, our dignity.

But let's focus on the management part of *pain management* for a minute. I think there are two definitions that apply here regarding the word management as it pertains to pain. One is the process of dealing with or controlling things or people. In this instance, it's about controlling pain. But there is an archaic definition of management that I think applies here. That definition is *trickery, deceit*.

And what about our emotions? When we consistently numb ourselves, we never grow emotionally. Why? Because emotional maturity requires that we deal with our painful stuff. Just as numbing physical pain does not heal the damage to our bodies, numbing ourselves against our hurts and hang-ups does not heal our wounded spirits. That is God's job. And He is the master restorer.

Quoting one of our staff pastors, Marty Jeanice, in Christ we don't have hang-ups. We have "hang-ons" because God will heal us of all we choose to let go of. We just must let Him.

Are you with me? Good.

What about that trickery and deceit?

Well... It's a lie to believe that any kind of emotional high, even the feel-goods we get at church, will make us instantly better.

The Feel-Good Preacher

Some preachers feel the same pressure the doctors feel. He must help the patient, but the patient has only one thing on his mind: "make this pain go away." The preacher finds himself spending more time trying to help the churchgoer feel good while never having the freedom to give any real-life solutions. The churchgoer becomes a user of the system instead of a part of the functioning body we call the church.

We need the music to speak to our agony. The preacher needs to understand our pain and prescribe words that numb the pain because the idea of really having spiritual therapy just seems too slow and, well, painful.

I would encourage anyone reading this book to believe me when I say that Jesus can and will set us free from the sinful dysfunctions of our life. But His goal is not to just numb our pain so that we don't have to feel it anymore. Why not? Because numbing pain allows us to feel fine when the injury is still there. God's plan for us is true healing. Not just to look okay on the outside, but to be whole and healthy where it counts, on the inside. And what is happening on the inside will then be evident on the outside.

What does a quick fix look like? Well, it's not always obvious.

It can look like wanting out of a relationship because getting along is going to require painful change. We say "I do" but never think through on all the possible "do's" that might come our way.

Or maybe it's looking for agreement with our bad thought processes and unhealthy opinions. We don't want to feel bad about our bad attitude. We want to feel justified.

Or, this is a big one: we want approval for our sexual immorality. Regardless of if it's multiple partners or a monogamous sexual relationship outside of marriage, we don't want anyone questioning our lack of self-control and commitment.

The quick fixes leave us with short-term peace that is later replaced by more pain than we originally felt. Eventually, the things in church that used to numb us from our pain and dysfunction are not enough. We have become immune to the usual dose of church and we begin to scream for more hyped-up feel-good vibes. We discard true "spiritual therapy" as an option.

I know this may seem a little bit "in your face". Just stay with me. At least until the next chapter.

Facing the Giant

My heart was saddened the day I heard of a friend found dead in his Jacuzzi. He was a nice guy, and yes, a Christian. Something that started out as a prescription to manage the pain from a back injury turned into years of prescription drug addiction. Sure, the masking of his pain helped him to function, in the beginning. But when nothing about his condition received a permanent fix, his life *in all areas* began to deteriorate.

Take notice that nothing in his life was made better by this method of pain management. An area of pain never stays put. It bleeds, radiates to other areas. He needed what he thought was a "fix," only to find out that he wasn't fixing anything. He went from a damaged back to a damaged life. One problem led to many others.

> An area of pain never stays put. It bleeds, radiates to other areas.

Until one day, his heart stopped while he was in his hot tub. Doing what?

Trying to make the pain from that same nagging back injury subside…

I'm not trying to demonize good doctors who are simply trying to help a patient in intense pain. Thank God not everyone who is prescribed pain pills becomes an addict. Though I do think it happens more than it should.

I wonder if church has become a place where we create more problems than we fix. We train people to need church in an unhealthy manner. We teach them to want church but fail to help them to gain spiritual health. The church was meant to facilitate health; it was not meant to addict us to programs or personalities. We find ourselves with a "fiend" for church but have little knowledge of God. We are addicted to the emotional "feel goods" we get by going to church, doing our duty, and checking a task off our list while failing to see we still have unhealthy thought processes resulting in poor life choices that hinder us from obtaining genuine life-changing spiritual health.

As a pastor, I believe church is truly the hope of the world. It is the place where Jesus is preached. It is a place to find hope and peace. It is a place to learn about the solution to our greatest problem, sin. Sin is the enemy. To diagnose the problem as anything else is total negligence by the church and especially the preachers. We must face our issues and realize that simply numbing the pain won't fix anything.

To sing songs that make us feel good is fine until it is only a method of escape. Being encouraged is healthy until we refuse to be challenged as well. God loves His church and all the emotionally gratifying experiences that come along with it, if we are willing to take responsibility and face our challenges as well.

I believe in the anesthesia of humor, creativity, stories, and other methods preachers use to communicate God's Word. I use them myself. These methods are necessary because all spiritual surgeries can only be done with anesthesia. I also believe in encouragement and support. God designed all of these to help the believer to pursue a healthy relationship with Him.

> If we actively pursue getting better and stronger in God, we won't just love the good feelings we get from attending, we will also grow closer to God and have the life of genuine redemption God intended for us.

If we actively pursue getting better and stronger in God, we won't just love the good feelings we get from attending, we will also grow closer to God and have the life of genuine redemption God intended for us.

The Tickle Monster

There is a popular children's book by Josie Bissett called *Tickle Monster*. It's about a loveable monster who has just flown in from Planet Tickle. The monster's mission is to tickle any child who happens to be following along with the Tickle Monster storyline. The goal is for parent/child time with parents reading aloud and tickling their kiddos and said kiddos giggling and squirming and having fun. It promotes great bonding moments.

Want to know what's not so great?

Adults who attend church looking for the alien from Planet Tickle. Sorry to disappoint, but I'm not that guy.

> *"For the time will come when people will not put up with sound doctrine. Instead, to suit their own desires, they will gather around them a great number of teachers to say what their itching ears want to hear."*
> 2 Timothy 4:3 NIV

This is so sobering to me. To realize that one of the signs that we are experiencing the end of the world as we know it is that men would want to have their ears tickled instead of hearing the truth of God's Word. To preach about freedom without confronting sin, to preach peace without war, to preach encouragement without challenge, to preach heaven without hell, to preach relationships without purity, to preach Jesus without commitment is some of what is happening to the church by its own version of Planet Tickle. The Tickle Monster has no place in God's church and the Church Junkies must beware.

Strange Things

Why has church been so good for some, while for others it seems to have only made them worse? A similar question is why some can leave a hospital on their way to recovery, and others seem to only get worse with the same sickness. They can both have the same issues, but each responded differently to the treatment. One wants his back to get healthier, while the other just wants to feel better right now. One wants to learn to deal with the pain and function the best she can, while the other won't look past the immediate "fix."

Good News

The good news about Jesus Christ.
> *"Now, brothers and sisters, I want you to remember the Good News I told you. You received that Good News message, and you continue to base your life on it. That Good News, the message you heard from me, is God's way to save you. But you must continue believing it. If you don't, you believed for nothing."*
> 1 Corinthians 15:1-2 ERV

The church is the bearer of good news. Every news station you turn to is getting your attention by being the bearer of bad news. They are trying to shock and appall so that you don't change the channel or click off their website.

It's called drama.

The church is none of that, or at least isn't supposed to be. It is a movement that has only good news. Even when the Word of God, or the preacher, confronts your behavior or thinking it is all for your benefit and to point you in the direction of health and fulfillment.

Baby Boomers, Generation X, Generation Y, Millennials, and any other generation you can categorize all have their own understanding of life. I see an overlapping consistent trend in our current society that transcends age and generational trends. I call it Generation Medication. If we gain weight, there is a pill for it. If we can't sleep, there is a pill for it. If we are having a bad day, a couple of drinks at the club will unwind us. If our parents are getting on our nerves, drugs are readily available to escape from the pressure of responsibility. If our kids are misbehaving, there are "calm down" pills for that. There is medication for everything. The days of doing it the hard way seem to be fading into the world of make-believe where you can take a pill, a smoke, or a drink for just about anything.

Denial

I was recently working out in a hotel gym when I heard about a music artist getting arrested for DUI. His mug shot seemed to confirm his charge. He looked like a young guy who was strung out on drugs. My heart always goes out to these young men and women who get trapped in that lifestyle; however, this was a unique case.

He was caught driving while high and his friends, family, and police all agreed he had a problem, and yet he said in an interview that he had an eating disorder, not a drug problem.

During the interview, he denied being a drug addict and almost in the same breath admitted to three prescription drugs he was taking, all of which were strong medications. These were helping him to cope but not to thrive. I refuse to accept that as the norm. You should too.

Just where does the church fit into a world that is looking for a quick fix? How do we get people to live healthy lives while slowly getting better? The world is offering a quick fix that leads to a long road of broken. The problem is the method used to fix one issue often results in other issues that then require more medications. The cycle is never ending. It reminds me of the Jeff Foxworthy joke in which he pretends to be a prescription medication commercial with a ridiculously long and painful list of side effects that clearly outweigh the benefits.

The church was meant to heal the sickness of sin not mask it. Let's look at what the prophet Isaiah said about Jesus and His church:

> "The Spirit of the Lord GOD is upon me, Because the LORD has anointed me to bring good news to the afflicted; He has sent me to bind up the brokenhearted, to proclaim liberty to captives and freedom to prisoners;"
>
> Isaiah 61:1 NASB

That's right, the church was meant to give people Jesus and Jesus would heal our damaged lives. Our broken hearts would be put back together and have new hope. The falsely accused and oppressed could turn to Him and find help in a time of need. Those bound by spirits of darkness, imprisoned by fear and any other addiction or emotion would have freedom. How? To reference John 8:36, *"he that the son hath set free is free indeed."*

It's understandable that we are tempted to self-medicate or convince a doctor to medicate us. It's what we know. I'm not a person who believes that medication is a sin or going to the doctor says that you don't have faith. I'm saying that we are looking for healing from other sources that can only come from Jesus. Any other avenue may appear to work in the short term but will not work in the long term.

Before Jesus was crucified, do you remember what He said He would leave? That's right, peace.

> *"I leave you peace. It is my own peace I give you. I give you peace in a different way than the world does. So don't be troubled. Don't be afraid."*
>
> John 14:27 ERV

We don't know what we don't know. While we are looking to fix the obvious, God is looking at the root. Until the moment we acknowledge God and turn to Him and His Word for reference we will be trying to fix something with useless methods. When we bring our old ways of coping to church and insist on applying them as we always have, refusing to think there may be something we don't know, we are setting ourselves up for failure. We cry that church just didn't help us. Is it that church has not helped us? Or have we undermined our own deliverance and healing by refusing to think that there may be something we don't know? We apply old thought patterns to new concepts and come up with bogus results.

Epic failure. Again.

Just hold on, though, all is not lost. God is, after all, the Redeemer. To redeem is to compensate for the faults or bad aspects of something. Or in this case someone a.k.a. YOU.

The Church is the hospital that has the Great Physician known as Jesus Christ. If you are tired of the disappointment of failed attempts to gain healing, I recommend you take heart and try a healthy church that allows Jesus to do what only He can do.

> **When we bring our old ways of coping to church and insist on applying them as we always have, refusing to think there may be something we don't know, we are setting ourselves up for failure.**

> "Not by might nor by power, but by my spirit saith the LORD of Hosts."
> Zechariah 4:6 KJV

> "And ye shall know the truth, and the truth shall make you free."
> John 8:32 KJV

"Through church, I have dealt with years of fear because of learned misconceptions of God. However, because of church I have also received hope, freedom from fear, and a healthy understanding of God and His love."

- Tony

2
CHURCH REHAB

Hello, my name is Josh and I'm a Church Junkie.

Yes, there have been many times in my life I have fallen into the category of going to church for the quick fix. My addiction to church hasn't been all bad. In fact, there has been a lot more good than bad. With that being said, I believe it is time for some changes in the church world. We, the church, need to check ourselves into God's Rehabilitation Clinic and let God Himself restructure our thoughts and behaviors concerning church.

Most of us know about church or have at least gone to church a few times. It's been my observation that America is pretty educated on Jesus and what He did on the cross for the sins of humanity. And though you may not know a great deal I venture to say you probably know at least a little something or have heard a rumor or two.

However, what if I told you that most of our ideas of church come from people rather than the One who invented the concept of church? What if I told you that something meant to glorify God and bless His people has become something strangely different?

It feels strange just to write those words. Every preacher I know and every church attendee I know would deny that accusation, as would I. When we go to church, who are our thoughts on? Are they on Jesus? Or are they on what we need or what is needed from us?

What is the church?

In Scripture we find the origination of the church. Jesus came to pay the price for the sins of all mankind and to reestablish relationship with them. He spoke of this news as the good news, the gospel. This whole idea is so exciting. An all-knowing, all-powerful creator wanting to show mercy and grace to people who don't deserve it. This news was meant to heal and unite people around Jesus Christ our Messiah. He let us know that He would return to heaven but would send the Holy Spirit to live inside believers; they would unite around the truth of the good news and share it with everyone around them. This was the birth of the church. (Acts 2, 8, 10, 19)

So how did we get so off track as to think that church is about denominations, music styles, preaching styles, pews vs. chairs, steeples, days of the week to meet, leadership positions, how much money to give, how many people are attending, and all the other things that pose as church? It's no wonder fewer people are going to church. It might not be church they are actually avoiding...

According to a 2015 article on the website outreachmagazine.com, "7 Startling Facts: An Up Close Look at Church Attendance in America", written by Kelly Shattuck and appearing in ChurchLeaders online magazine, only 17.7 percent of Americans attend church.[1]

The rapid reduction in church attendance is not a reflection of culture unless you believe culture rules the church. I believe that every good dance team has one who is in the lead. Does culture lead the church or church the culture? Whoever leads this dance gets the blame or credit for its performance. My case is that we need thinking rehabilitation as to what leads to a drift from church attendance. The drift from church attendance is in direct correlation to the decline in cultural morals.

As Christians, we say we are sick of the cultural trends of immorality and the breakdown of the family unit; however, we haven't really associated that decline to our lack of ability to convince our world that Jesus is the answer. We know that Jesus is a perfect Savior. So why don't people want our Jesus? Why don't they come to church with us and learn about Him?

It reminds me of the mother who raised a good boy and can tell stories of his kindness and goodwill. She can vouch that the boy she raised was a good person; however now he is a drug addict. He got mixed up in the wrong crowd and now needs rehab. That is the same description the church had in its infant stage. It was pure, and it was powerful, but somehow got mixed up in the wrong crowd. I believe the church, as a whole, is still the best thing going in the world, but it desperately needs rehab.

We, the church, must get back to Biblical church as God intended it, not our cultural attempts to include God in our lives through religion. When Jesus is put back as the centerpiece of our faith and everything else revolves around that truth, the structure we call the church will become stronger than ever. Despite its need for rehab the church is still the greatest and longest-lasting organization that exists in the world today.

Reasons Not to Not Go to Church

I know I am being very direct in my approach here, but it is my hope that you are tired of the world speaking in code so that no one hurts anyone's feelings.

Yeah, that was a warning sentence, so I don't hurt your feelings with the next few statements. I'm a nice guy like that. You're welcome.

The truth here is that numbers are declining, and they tell the story of a country that is going to church less and less. We are choosing other events, clubs, activities, and leisure instead of gathering with other believers to worship Jesus.

I have asked many people over the years why they have stopped going to church. The answers sound something like this:

The pastor really hurt my feelings.
They did not even notice me.
There are hypocrites in that church.
All they want is my money.
I didn't like the preaching.
I didn't like the music.

I could go on, but I won't as the list is extensive. And if I leave someone's pet peeve out, they are sure to get their feelings hurt and stop going to church…

Not the Real Reason

Have you ever asked someone what was wrong and they answered you, but you knew it wasn't the real problem? Like a child that pretends a part of their body is hurting when really their feelings are hurt because you didn't let them have something they wanted.

The real reasons we don't go to church as often as other generations are difficult to conclude. We use a lot of clichés that sound acceptable and true until we really look at them.

What do I mean by that?

Well, most of us shop at places in which we don't even know the owners. We eat at restaurants where we don't meet the cooks. We pull for sports teams in which we don't know one person in the front office. We have opinions about those places and people, but none of that stops us from supporting or attending. We allow for human error even if it frustrates us. When a CEO of Apple makes a decision we disagree with, we just let out a few words or thoughts of frustration and continue using our iMac, iPad, iPhone, and any other Apple product we buy.

But when it comes to the church, whoa boy! I see a different standard applied to the church world. I see us as being completely intolerant of any mistakes a person in leadership makes. If a pastor ignored us, we leave. If a preacher offended us, we never go back. If the music was too loud, we look for another church or stop going all together.

Have you ever stopped to wonder why it is so easy to be hard on the church but forgiving to less-meaningful institutions? Is it possible that we are holding the church up to an unfair standard to excuse a much deeper problem within ourselves? Why do we expect more from church folks, at church, than we do church folks at the supermarket? Are we expecting them to be something other than what they are just because they are at the "house of God"? That's like saying it is okay for sick people to be sick at Walmart but it's unacceptable for them to be sick at the hospital.

> **Is it possible that we are holding the church up to an unfair standard to excuse a much deeper problem within ourselves?**

You see, I believe most of us would agree that Jesus is greater than a computer. That God is more powerful than our favorite sports team. And yes, our pastor or preacher is a better man than most of the CEOs of the companies from which we faithfully buy our products. So why do we do this?

I propose that we have done this since we were kids. It started with our parents. We received shelter from them, love from them, and a plethora of other benefits; however, we looked up to our irresponsible uncle or some other person we deified while belittling our parents. In other words, we crucify the people who love us most while celebrating those who put an exceedingly small investment into our lives.

Forgive me for being so blunt, but is this a failure on our part to "grow up"?

The Blame Game and Other Sad Tales

We all have that one sibling, friend, neighbor, or spouse that seems to blame everything they do on someone or something other than themselves. I grew up in a church culture where everything bad was the devil. If you were struggling in your finances, it was because the devil attacked your money. It was never because you didn't budget or work hard on the job so you could make more money. It was always the devil. I'm inclined to believe the devil was in awe of how much credit he got for things he didn't cause.

Could it be our own immaturity causing our dysfunction? Before you dismiss that question, take a break, get a snack and read on.

The immature do not want to be responsible for anything, especially their eternal well-being. One of the clear marks of maturity is responsibility. It's having the resources to take care of ourselves emotionally, physically, and yes, spiritually.

When we were young, we didn't pay bills, count calories, or solve real-world problems. We just wanted to know when the next video game was coming out, where our friends were buying their clothes, and what could be put on our faces to stop those ugly bumps from interfering with our social life.

It is in maturation that we began to want to pay our bills, take responsibility for our actions, and yes, even count calories. I see a trend of immaturity in our world that makes us all want to stay children even when we become adult age. Dr. Tim Elmore says that twenty-six years old is the new eighteen.[2] We don't want to grow up. We view it as a bad thing. As children we had it so good that we have no desire to become adults.

My parents were from the old school. We didn't tell them how it was going to be (not if we wanted a healthy rear end). We looked forward to the day we could make our own decisions and choices. What I see today is a "failure to launch" mentality in adults.

Failure to Launch

It is common today for our children to never grow up. We feed them, give them shelter, possibly even send them to college and yet, they return home to stay with Mom and Dad with little to no motivation to be different. Who wouldn't want to stay under the safety and provision of their parents? Dirty clothes magically appear back in our rooms clean and folded. There are food and utilities to be absorbed with none of the pressure it takes to make those things available. And, the biggest miracle of all is that no demands are made on us at all. Nirvana indeed.

I often wonder what made parents begin to coddle children so much so that they never want to become independent adults. How did our love become so misguided? We have stunted their development in our efforts to love and support them.

I'm certainly not claiming to have all the answers to these questions, but to provide a little insight, here is my take: we have redefined love to the detriment of those needing our love the most. We have narrowed love into an idea of giving our children what they want instead of what they need. We have defined love as giving children little to no adversity in a misguided effort to protect them. We have gone to extremes to insure they experience no emotional strain.

So, what's wrong with that?

Well, it is adversity and pain that brings the maturity needed to be responsible for ourselves. It is possible that we thought that if we protected and provided for our children in these capacities that they would just end up being great adults. Instead we made the nest so comfortable that we took away their desire to fly.

Prepare for Takeoff

We go to my parents' house several times a year. We are fed, loved on, reminded of the importance of family. It is a safe place. It is a good place to go; however, it is not a place that is meant to be a substitute for having my own home. It isn't meant to be a staying place or a substitute for my own ability to rest in Christ for my provision. It is the place I learned how to feed myself, lead, grow, and give, but it was never meant to be the place I relied on to the point of not maturing.

The same is with church. That building, that church service, wasn't meant to be our destiny, but rather a fuel stop for the journey to our destination. What kind of journey would we be on if all we ever did was travel from home to the gas station? The journey of the Christian is about heaven and the relationship we have with Jesus and each other. If heaven is our destination and this life is the journey we take to get there, then why are we stuck at the gas station (church without purpose) or, for some, never even leaving home to fuel up?

> We love the church and feel fed and loved when we go, but never realize that we were meant to become *something* from the experience.

Church can become similar in that we never grow up in God. We love the church and feel fed and loved when we go, but never realize that we were meant to become something from the experience.

People who don't have the ability to receive correction only look for encouragement. Encouragement without correction produces and reproduces irresponsibility. Encouragement is rendered ineffective without correction. Encouragement receives its power from the balance and perspective of the possibility of needing correction. Without black, white loses its meaning. Without bad, good loses its value. Without darkness, light loses its purpose. Encouragement needs its partner Correction like Sonny needed Cher, Pippen needed Jordan, and Jonah needed the whale.

I believe more in encouragement than correction. Once a problem is identified, healthy correction, if received properly, brings change.

John Maxwell says affirmation comes before confrontation.[3] What does that mean? It means healthy correction begins with trust and trust is formed from a positive relationship between both the corrected and the corrector. Bottom line? We don't take correction from people we don't respect and trust.

The method I use is healthy correction, and then implementing consistent encouragement as the person or organization pursues the goal to which the correction pointed toward. There is no shame in falling or in needing help to get up.

It is also relevant to understand the purpose of church leadership. The primary purpose and function of the leadership of the church (pastor, teacher, evangelist, prophet, and apostle) is to prepare the church (its people) for the working of ministry. If all church becomes is a *provision* and never a *preparation*, we create a spiritual climate in which we coddle but never launch. There is nothing wrong with any of that until we are unable to feed ourselves. We must mature beyond our tendency to go to church to "get" for self as opposed to going to church to "give" of self to others.

> We must mature beyond our tendency to go to church to "get" for self as opposed to going to church to "give" of self to others.

Real Church

If you know your church history, you are painfully aware that once the church was legalized, it got organized… What began as unexplainable became institutional. The *ekklesi* [church] would find itself wrestling with a question we continue to wrestle with today…who is the ekklesi for? - *Deep and Wide* by Andy Stanley[4]

Should sick people go to a hospital? Seems like a silly question but let me ask it in church language. Should sinners go to church? I believe the answer is yes. I believe that is the answer that Jesus would give as well. In fact, He said that the reason He came was for the sinner.

We all like going to places where we feel accepted. This is why mothers get all the "Hi Mom" TV time from college athletes. Mom loves us no matter what. She makes the "real" us feel accepted and loved. The church should be the same kind of place, and maybe that's the selling point for the church. All are welcome in God's government. Whatever the condition of your life today, the church is the place for you. God's church is designed to help everyone in every situation.

I hear people say all the time that they hate going to the doctor or hospital. I'll give you my theory on that. Every time we go there it is because we are sick, and we get bad news, or at least it seems like bad news. However, if we are sick, it is imperative that we go to get healing. It is the same with church. If we are struggling and spiritually sick, it is imperative that we seek spiritual health from the right source. Even if it means we must hear the bad news that something is wrong. There will be "good news" that comes with it as well as instruction on what to do with the news we received. As to our spiritual self, as long as there is life, there is hope. (Ecclesiastes 9:3-5 (paraphrased).)

Walk-Ins Welcome

When I was in elementary school, my dad used to take me to a local barbershop called LARODAN. LArry, ROy and DAN were the proprietors. It was the kind of place you would see in a movie. One of them was the personality. Then there was the cigar guy who had that important yet mysterious look. He was a man of few words but lots of puffs. The final guy was bald. Yeah, I don't trust bald barbers either. A bald barber could be jealous of my hair and choose to scalp my blessing. Come to think of it, I walked out with very little hair on my head pretty much every time I got a haircut there...

I think what my dad liked about this place (besides the fact that he could get inexpensive embarrassing haircuts for me) was that you could just walk in and get some hair help (help in this case is relative). I have vivid memories of the soda machine, the hair on the floor, and chairs of blue-collar men who were about to be scalped (especially by the bald guy).

The idea that they accepted anyone at any time is appealing to me. Especially after I read Scriptures like "God is no respecter of persons." in Acts 10:34 KJV or "...And whosoever will, let him take the water of life freely." in Revelation 22:17 KJV.

> God wants a church that will love anyone who wants to be loved by Him.

God wants a church that will love anyone who wants to be loved by Him. He isn't interested in a church that makes the outsider feel like they aren't good enough to come in. I don't mind a church that likes to look nice but is it possible we have become so "fashionable" that the ordinary person feels out of place? It is possible we have become so sophisticated that the "average Joe" doesn't want to come in the doors? Is it even possible that we have become so saved that the sinner doesn't feel confident to "walk in"?

House of Prayer is a church that strives to be that "walk-ins accepted" kind of place (without the cigar and the bad jokes). We know that not everyone will do what they need to do and make the necessary changes to follow Christ, but that doesn't stop us from opening the front door as wide as we possibly can because we believe in the concept that walk-ins are not just welcomed but accepted.

What happens once we are spiritually healthy, for those who can say, "I'm saved and don't have any major sin issues"? When we achieve a quality level of health we must actively pursue keeping and enhancing that health. We are free from the damage that sin executes because of the Great Physician (Jesus), but we must actively seek to maintain that health and pursue further health. If we are damaged and dysfunctional today, we don't have to stay that way. And once health is achieved, we must keep watch over the state of our health to maintain our peace and joy for all our tomorrows.

Fitting In

I have a son who is extremely athletic. He will play any and every sport I allow him. When he played soccer, I was his coach for a couple of seasons. I remember one time when I wore a pair of jeans that were a little too tight and a little too old. In the heat of the coaching moment when the team gathered around me for inspiration and instruction, I squatted down and *rrrrriiippp*! Yep, my pants tore. Not the kind of "I'll just stay standing and be okay" tear. It was the kind of tear that reveals your greatest fear regardless of how you stand. Little Tommy on the team grew eyes the size of basketballs. I totally lost the attention of the kids as they laughed and laughed and then laughed some more. To this day, he refers to me as the "underwear coach."

Our churches are in danger of becoming those kinds of pants. So old and tightly knit that the moment an outsider tries to get into our culture our seams come apart. We find ourselves unprepared to accommodate them and unwilling to change to receive them into our "inner circle."

If our church structure and ideas don't focus on allowing the broken sinners to "fit in" then our churches will eventually become irrelevant to the mission of Christ, which is "to save the sinner." When the sinner messes up your plan, you have the wrong plan. The plan that Jesus had is *for* sinners. The whole operation is centered on them. It's no big surprise that it wasn't outsiders who wanted Jesus crucified; it was the very people who were supposed to be waiting for Him. They missed Him because they wanted a Jesus that fit into their own concepts of a Savior, instead of realizing He came to help them fit into Him.

According to research, some of the greatest risk periods for drug abuse leading to addiction are during major life transitions. Another explanation is that of association with peers who abuse drugs. The need to fit in, to be part of a group, to not be alone, is integral to human interaction. As the church we must be welcoming to facilitate this intrinsic human need. We should acknowledge that humanity needs to fit in somewhere and the church should be that place. I refuse to be a part of a church with large buildings and small hearts. I believe that Jesus is asking His church to love people like He loves them. The kind of love that says, "come as you are, and we'll figure out the rest after that encounter".

Our hospitality teams and ministry leaders don't need to resemble TSA workers who frisk, scan, and suspect everyone of misconduct. We need open-heart policies and functions that allow every kind of person to walk in and feel the love and hope that is in Jesus Christ our Lord and Savior. I pray that, as the church, we rehabilitate our functionalities to resemble that open-heart policy.

Right vs. Familiar

I desire a church that trades what is familiar and comfortable for what is right. People are messy and have issues. True church exists for them. The church should have a tension of standing for what's right while loving those who do wrong. The church should pursue holiness while loving those who are unholy.

> **People are messy and have issues. True church exists for them.**

Familiar is not always best. Some of the most common activities and church slangs exclude the outsider. We like them because we are familiar with them. Familiarity gives us a false sense of security. Like an abused person who stays in a dangerous and unhealthy relationship rather than explore the unfamiliar, we never realize that a better world exists beyond our current experience.

As Church Junkies, we are challenged to rethink the way we do church, view church and present the church. Our challenge is great, but the hope behind the challenge should inspire us to try.

There are millions of people looking for answers and they don't know where to find them. I pray we become beacons that light the path they should take. The church is the answer and we are the church. Come on church junkies, let's go get them and change the world. Jesus is with us!

"I grew up in church always feeling that when I was good God loved me and when I wasn't, He did not accept me. I have since learned, through church, how to live every day in God's love and acceptance."

- Judy

3
MORE THAN A BUILDING

The church I grew up in has a foundation rooted in spiritual values. I respect, and am grateful for, what I learned there. However, some of its practices I view as unacceptable.

I attended a private church school throughout my grade school years. It was a sheltered environment and I appreciate everything I was taught there. I graduated in the top eight of my senior class. There were eight of us.

When I was growing up, I didn't believe my friends, or their families, would want to come to my church. In fact, I don't remember ever bringing a friend to church while I was growing up! It wasn't because the love of Jesus was not preached there. It was. Or that the people that went to church there were terrible people. They weren't. Or that the pastor was a bad guy. He wasn't. My father was my pastor, and if ever there was a man that walks humbly before God, it is my dad. It wasn't that I didn't think my friends wouldn't accept the truths taught there; I just didn't believe they would understand some of its practices.

Policies over People

When it was time to go to college, I decided to attend Nicholls State University. It was a completely different world than the one I had previously known. At college, I met some guys who were a part of another denomination than the one to which I belonged. We became good friends and had lots of fun hanging out. I decided to muster up the courage to ask them to come to church with me. To my surprise, they agreed. I have never forgotten how that went down.

At that time, I played the drums for my church, so I explained to them that I would sit with them after I finished playing drums for the worship. In my heart I was hoping that these guys will love my church as much as I did and look past some of its weirdness. Yes, there was some weirdness. I even imagined they would choose my church to be their church.

But something very different happened.

You see, my church had a no-gum-chewing policy. The whys thereof, I do not know. However, it, apparently, was on the top of the priority list. My friends, because they were normal and had no idea that chewing gum was a church crime, came chomping like champs. One of our ushers felt it necessary to approach my friends about the gum chewing. Never mind that they were first-time guests and had no idea about the gum thing. So, Usher Guy approaches my friend and holds out his hand in front of my friend's mouth. My friend was clueless as to what the guy was doing until Usher Guy muttered one word, "*Gum!*" My friend politely spit his gum into Usher Guy's hand. Usher Guy walked away feeling accomplished. My friends walked away freaked out and never came back. It's pretty much impossible to explain away or justify that type of incident. I didn't even try.

Apparently, my friends aren't the only ones that come away with a less than appealing experience. In an article "It's Hard to Go to Church", which was published in *theAtlantic.com* on August 23, 2016, Emma Green writes:

Among people who were raised religiously and who fell away from religion in adult life, roughly one-fifth said their dislike of organized religion was the reason. Another 50 percent said they stopped believing in the particular tenets of the faith they were raised in. Insofar as the decline in U.S. religious affiliation is an intellectual or philosophical story, it seems to be this: Fewer people are willing to sign on with the rules and reputations of institutions that promote faith. That doesn't mean people don't care about religious ideas or questions—many of those who are unaffiliated with a particular group still consider themselves "religious" or "seeking"—but they might not be as sold on the religious institutions themselves.[1]

Wow! I must ask myself what part, if any, do we play in that kind of disillusionment.

I hold no grudges toward my church. And I realize that bad experiences happen everywhere. We were doing the best we knew at the time and one usher's skewed perception didn't represent everyone. It still hurts a little to think about it, though. My friends could have easily identified my church as an anti-gum-chewing organization. Years later I realize this was a case of putting policies and processes before people. At the time though, I experienced a bit of disillusionment myself. One thing this experience really helped me realize, though, is how we get these odd ideas about what a church is or isn't. My dad, as pastor, began the changing of these methods while keeping the message of the good news of the gospel, and today I pastor these same great people with the concept of "people first." Always.

Based on bad experiences some might say that church is a place that messed-up people go simply because the few people they know that go to church are in bad shape. Or, some may think church is a place where the pastor is a fraud because the one church they heard about had an unethical minister. It is my hope that anyone who might have a misunderstanding of church or has had a bad experience would give it another prayerful try.

For many of us, church is the answer to all of life's questions, not a building with a steeple. I love that about church. It is the place we should find love and acceptance in a world where love and acceptance can be sparse. This type of experience of church creates a necessary and healthy dependency on church. It is a true family, one that sticks by our side in our tough times and provides safety for when we need it. That is what a healthy family does for one other.

For some, though, it has become an enabler of unhealthy practices that create an even more unhealthy dependency on the church, when the church was meant to be a living, breathing organism that distributes life and peace with a *healthy* level of dependency.

Church was meant to be a representation of Christ Himself. Wikipedia seems to think that church is "a building used for Christian religious activities." Well, it's no wonder we are losing the value of church. If church was just a building used to practice religion, then why would I add that to my to-do list?

Jesus told us that He came to give life and to give it more abundantly. (John 10:10) We also learn in the Holy Scriptures that the followers of Christ were His representatives on earth. That's right! We, the church folks, are meant to be a life-giving body of believers that do what Jesus Himself had set out to do, give life.

Think about it! It is getting harder and harder to find hope, peace, love, safety, and all the other common qualities we desire for our lives. Jesus was saying that He is the answer to meeting these needs and the church is the facilitator of the relationship between God and us.

Though church has been radically and consistently changed in its methods and culture, its purpose has not wavered. We are the hope in a hopeless world. The church was a concept Scripture introduced to us as people who are called out of ordinary life into a life lived for God and His cause which is *"to seek and save that which was lost."* Luke 19:10 NASB

> **Though church has been radically and consistently changed in its methods and culture, its purpose has not wavered.**

And just in case you are still unclear about what was lost, it is the relationship between God and man. This connection will bring the answers to life's difficult questions. And it should be an amazing experience where we encounter the presence of God in such profound ways through worship and preaching, and of course, prayer.

Unhealthy Church

What is unhealthy church? One that creates junkies who are users of the church without having the true experience of what it means to be a member of God's family.

I once was that addict. "Hi, my name is Josh and I'm a church addict." Yeah, I know, it has the feel of an AA member declaration, only the addiction is church. It gets easy to go for the "fix" and leave, only to repeat the bad habits and experiences that brought us desperately to church last Sunday. Moving from church service to church service like a drug addict moves from fix to fix, we are desperately missing the opportunity to experience the true purpose of gathering together in the common belief that God will meet us there. And that something special will happen. For us.

> *"This is true because if [[L For where] two or three people ·come [are assembled/gathered] together in my name, I am there with them [among them; in their midst]."*
>
> Matthew 18:20 EXB

We can easily become church addicts because we feel a deep need to escape the realities of life without giving a thought to allowing God to change our hearts and our behaviors. And so, church becomes a drug of sorts. We come to church to numb the pain of life only to feel it even stronger when the high is over.

Can you relate to this?

> **We feel so messed up and are trying to escape, looking for the answer and not looking to be part of the solution.**

We feel so messed up and are trying to escape, looking for the answer and not looking to be part of the solution. Why? Because we don't believe we are qualified to be part of the solution. We think we are too messed up.

I want you to come away from here with some ideas on how to break the unhealthy cycles of going to church and instead find how church is meant to be a healthy and meaningful experience. If you ever get into the life-giving rhythms of experiencing God daily, the gathering of believers (and non-believers) will be a healthy experience instead of an unhealthy emotional fix that contributes to the confusion from which you are seeking to break free.

We are trying to escape the world as opposed to being the hope in the world. The struggles of life don't leave us regardless of our medicine of choice: alcohol, drugs, sex, church (in the non-healthy sense), etc. The church was meant to overcome the world because Jesus overcame it.

> **The church was meant to overcome the world because Jesus overcame it.**

Jesus Himself confirms it in John 16:33: *"These things I*

have spoken to you, that in Me you may have peace. In the world you will have tribulation; but be of good cheer, I have overcome the world." ᴺᴷᴶⱽ

Church is intended to facilitate what should be a LIFE experience, not a once-a-week social engagement.

In my research it became clear to me that people aren't rejecting God, but merely the concept that the church building is the place that represents God. Thank God that church is more than a building. It is the Hope of the World.

"Growing up going to church was simply religion and a part of the routine. As I have gotten older, I've realized church is just another opportunity to meet with the God that loves me so much, that is what has kept me going my entire life."

- Shane

4
THE SIN ISSUE

When I was just a young boy, I remember listening to the LA Lakers play in the NBA playoffs on the radio in the 1980s. I didn't grow up with TV, so listening was my only option if I wasn't at my grandparents' house where I could watch a game on their TV. That was my earliest memory of hearing the name Magic Johnson.

Johnson was diagnosed HIV positive in 1991. Sports fans were devastated. I remember being in disbelief that Magic was going to eventually die of AIDS. However, Magic was still enjoying a vibrant life in business and sport endeavors as of 2017. "The only time I think about the disease is the two times a day I have to take my meds," he has been quoted as saying.

This is what Magic said in a 2015 article by Mathew Rodriguez addressing the question of if he still had HIV.

"I'm glad you brought this up, because first of all I do have it and have had it for 22 years. It's just laying asleep in my body. The drugs have done their part and I've done

my part by exercising and having a positive attitude about having HIV," Johnson explained. He goes on and says this, *"The same 30-something drugs are available to everybody else. I'm on three of them,"* Johnson said.[1]

Think about it, the resources exist to stop the disease, but people can't get to them. The disease progression may be stopped if one has the resources to pay for it. But good news about Jesus! Whereas good medication can help some, God medication can help all. And the access is readily available to everyone, no exceptions!

Paul wrote in a letter to the Romans around 57-58 AD that sin has this effect on us unless we take the antidote:

> *"For the wages of sin is death, but the free gift of God is eternal life through Christ Jesus our Lord."*
> Romans 6:23 NLT

Sin is a deadly virus. We are born with it.

> *"Indeed, we felt we had received the sentence of death. But this happened that we might not rely on ourselves but on God, who raises the dead."*
> 2 Corinthians 1:9 NIV

The church is the conduit, the I.V. if you will, with the antidote on hand to prevent people from dying of the sin disease.

> *"For the wages of sin is death, but the gift of God is eternal life."*
> Romans 6:23 NIV

Like HIV, sin left unattended will eventually destroy life. The potential of sin is in all of us.

If the church doesn't see itself as the distributors of the antidote to sin, then it will not assume responsibility for finding these sick people and bringing them to Jesus, the Great Physician. (Matthew 9:12, Mark 2:17, Luke 5:31).

What would happen if Magic sometimes missed those treatments? If he wasn't faithful to take those meds as prescribed? What if he only took his meds on Sundays? He would most certainly be giving his body over to a disease that is now contained and managed.

Sin is endemic to humanity. All of humanity shares this common denominator.

When we seek Jesus daily through prayer and His Word, the Bible, we find ourselves overcoming the sin that lives within us. Some may be tempted to say that they no longer deal with sin because they are saved, but this is what the apostle John said about the saved person having sin in them:

> *"If we say that we have no sin, we deceive ourselves, and the truth is not in us"*
> 1 John 1:8 KJV

We have the sin virus, but a consistent dose of Jesus prevents it from ruling and ruining our lives.

God always shows up when people in sincerity show up to worship Him. When we gather to seek Him and learn about Him, He promises in His Word to show up. The Jesus that we worship, pray to, love, believe in, read about, and preach about is the antidote to the virus called sin. He took the poison of thousands of generations and gave us the medicine of forgiveness and healing.

If most people believe church is a building that opens on Sunday for an hour or so, then yeah, I realize why the value of church is diminishing. Think about it, what important business would only open for a couple of hours a week? Especially if it was offering a necessary serum for a disease that is spreading daily…

That's right, if the church is the facilitator of Jesus' love and life, then it is the antidote to sin and destruction. We live in a world that's getting worse. The diseases are getting out of control. Especially when you realize that depression, addiction, divorce, loneliness, hopelessness, anger, violence, sexual misconduct, and all the other life-destroying commonalities we battle in our world are forms of diseases that the Bible calls sin and its results.

As healthy believers we must understand that our natural body contains the virus called sin, but with Jesus living inside of us, we will not die from it. Instead, we will be free from its power to kill us.

However, when we overemphasize the building and its programs, instead of the purpose and the message, we create zombie Christians who only come to life that one hour on Sunday (maybe a little longer for the churches with long-winded preachers). We can do better than this. And we should.

> *"Then desire when it has conceived gives birth to sin, and sin when it is fully grown brings forth death."*
>
> James 1:15 ESV

Sin is simply missing the mark of God's expectations. It is the poisonous desires that disobey the Word and will of God. Yes, sin is in us even if we are no longer sinners. It is just in remission. (Acts 2:38) Magic Johnson can live a healthy and full life. He can die an old man; however, he can never think he doesn't have HIV or give in to the temptation to stop taking the required medication that stops the HIV virus from becoming AIDS.

We are like that as believers. We are saved, and Jesus will protect us, lead us, and forgive us. But if we ever think we aren't susceptible to sin anymore, we will stop taking our daily medication of Bible reading, prayer, and godly relationships.

And what about that commission to share the antidote with others who don't have it yet?

Free Clinics

I'm from the South. It's hot. Really, it's not just hot. It's H-O-T hot. It's the kind of hot that produces sweat just by stepping outside. The months of June–September are especially hot, but we have been known to wear shorts and flip-flops for Christmas. Yes, really.

I was in college studying finance when this church friend of mine approached me with an idea of me running his mobile snowball stand (snow cone to those of you who live north of me). I remember laughing and thinking why would I ever want to pull a mobile snowball unit into neighborhoods and embarrass myself with that circus music.

I wasn't very sold on the idea, but I have always been a little adventurous and money was tight in those days. Eventually, I took the job and realized I was onto something. I got good at finding people outside and convincing them that they wanted some deliciously flavored shaved ice. I made twice as much as I was making at my previous job. It was fun.

I eventually bought two of my own mobile stands and hired one of my friends to run the one I wasn't running. I was on my way to "building my empire" in the words of Fred G. Sanford. Or so I thought (I didn't know I was a preacher yet).

One day I was driving through a neighborhood and the Spirit of God spoke so strong to my heart. He said, "I want to mobilize my church." I immediately knew what He was saying. You see, a mobile snowball stand sells two to three times the number of snowballs as a stationary stand because a stationary stand depends on people coming to it. A mobile stand goes to the customer. I could sell to the elderly who didn't drive anymore. I could go to the birthday parties. I could even help the mom who didn't want to get out with the kids that day. It was working, and I was learning. I made a lot of money selling snowballs, but I think the real purpose of that experience was to learn the value of taking what I had and bringing it to those that didn't have it.

> **They are rejecting our religious organizations; they are rejecting our building and service programs. But they still desperately need Jesus.**

People are going to church less and less, statistics say, but their need for God is just as great as it has always been. They are rejecting our religious organizations; they are rejecting our building and service programs. But they still desperately need Jesus. When we, the Church Junkies, stop building buildings only to think that people will magically appear and realize that we must mobilize our distribution of this good news, we can get back in the fight and start gaining ground for the church.

In 2017, George P. Wood wrote an article for *Influence Magazine* concerning the benefits a society gains from those that attend church. He cites missiologist Donald McGavran's catchphrase "redemption and lift" to explain that the good news of the redemption granted us by God lifts us from where we are and makes our lives better. And that the truth of God's Word engages the whole person: the *head* (our patterns of thought), the *heart* (our patterns of feeling), and the *hands* (our patterns of action and relationship). A person renewed by the gospel increasingly acts in a self-controlled and selfless manner rather than in a self-serving one, and this produces positive change in their material circumstances.[2]

McGavran's experiences and subsequent conclusions find comparative evidence in the research and statistics presented by sociologist Rodney Stark, in his book, *America's Blessings: How Religion Benefits Everyone, Including Atheists*. Stark states that compared to those who are less religious and irreligious, churchgoers are less likely to commit crimes, drop out of school, or commit suicide. And they are more likely to be employed, perform better on tests, be happy with and faithful to their spouses, have more satisfying sex lives, have better health (mental and physical), volunteer their time, and contribute to charities.[3]

Do I believe this to be true? Yes, I do, and I have, in fact, witnessed it time after time in the lives of those I pastor and in the good that is produced in our community from those whose circumstances have been lifted by their redemption.

There should come a time in everyone's walk with the Lord that we move beyond ourselves. When our needs are not so acute that we are bleeding out and in danger of expiring. It becomes time to pay it forward. We "self-health" when we reach toward those who are without to share what we have learned about God and the good news and what it has done for us.

So, having said all of this, I pray that you realize that being the church is more than just going to a building, though that is important. It's about being ready and able to facilitate the good news to those without it. It's like a spiritual free clinic on wheels, or in this case, legs. And we have the knowledge to dispense the scriptural antidote to the masses to help them get free from their endemic sin. Just as people may avoid hospitals because of what they may represent or experiences they have had or heard about, people may also avoid church. And sometimes when their health forces them to act, it is too late. We, the church, are like mobile clinics in that we can share the life-giving power of Jesus with anyone anywhere, and it's free! If going to church does not morph into the church going to those not going to church, then non-attenders will never see the richness

> **We "self-health" when we reach toward those who are without to share what we have learned about God and the good news and what it has done for us.**

that faithful church attendance will add to their lives. Jesus told His disciples this when going out and offering the healing power of this Gospel:

> *"...freely ye have received, freely give."*
> Matthew 10:8 KJV

"Most of my church life was about dressing my best and acting my best, always striving to portray what I thought I was supposed to be. But now I see when transparency replaces pretense in the church souls are healed and made whole."

— Jeff

5
RED PEN THEOLOGY

"Add not to His words, lest He reprove you, and you be found a liar."

Proverbs 30:6 AMP

I preach a lot. I feel like preaching is my way of obeying God and pleasing Him. I'm often reminded of the exchange between Peter and Jesus when Jesus kept asking Peter if Peter loved Him. Every time Jesus asked the question, Peter would answer correctly and then Jesus would say, "Feed my sheep." In other words, *give my people the words of life that they need to survive.*

I can be honest and say that there is some spontaneity to public speaking if you have my speaking style. Yes, I work off the script quite a bit, but I believe in making room for the leading of God's Spirit.

One day, I was preaching at House of Prayer and trying to get the congregation to understand the difference between the truth of God's Word and the customs and traditions we tag onto those truths. I said that if you were holding a red pen when you were saved, the tendency is to tell everyone they must be holding a red pen to receive Jesus. I called it the red pen theology. Churches are full of red pen theology and it keeps away those who have no use for red pens.

> **Churches are full of red pen theology and it keeps away those who have no use for red pens.**

When we come to the saving knowledge of Jesus Christ, it is so incredibly life changing. It's exciting and leaves an imprint on our thinking and behaviors. Forever.

When my parents were filled with the Spirit of God, they never looked back. They were willing to do anything, go anywhere, and believed everything that was told them. They were hungry for more of God once they had tasted of the truth of Jesus Christ. They were the personification of:

> "O taste and see that the LORD is good: blessed is the man that trusteth in him."
> Psalms 34:8 KJV

Whatever the church told my parents about living for God, they did it and with all their heart. I think it is the way we all should respond. What happens, though, when what we are told isn't in God's Word, or is at best a poor interpretation of Scripture?

Jesus said, "I am the way, the truth, and the life." John 14:6 KJV

That being said, I find that believers of all denominations have thrown in some things to go along with the Jesus truth. Those things we throw into the truth mix are the additions that religions and denominations are guilty of all over the world. They are the red pens of our religious experiences.

When we come to God for the first time, especially if we are the first generation in our family to really know Jesus as Lord and Savior, we are very open to the religious opinions of the people who lead us to Christ. We trust that they know what we don't know. This is not necessarily a bad thing. In fact, it's a natural thing. We tend to adopt the thinking and opinions of those who influence us the most, starting with our parents and then our peers and mentors. However, though we respect our influencers, it doesn't mean they are always right. Though we trust them to lead us…we must be students of the Word and the truths it holds so we form a foundation of belief based on our own relationship with Christ instead of living our lives based on what others have experienced.

> …we must be students of the Word and the truths it holds so we form a foundation of belief based on our own relationship with Christ instead of living our lives based on what others have experienced.

I once heard a story of a woman who gave her life to God and received the baptism of the Holy Spirit (Acts 2, 8,10,19) during an altar call, the invitation at the end of service to come forward to pray. After this wonderful experience, a well-intentioned member in the church began to discuss with her what "changes" she would have to now make to her lifestyle. The thing was, all the things Church Lady was telling Newbie were personal beliefs, not scriptural truths. These were Church Lady's red pens. Yes, a true salvation experience will be evidenced by a changed life, in thinking and lifestyle. However, we must never mistake or substitute those red pens for the scriptural truths of God's Word. That's not to say we shouldn't value and respect the extras that people do in their daily efforts to shed their old way of living. We should all find ways to acknowledge God in every aspect of our lives. It is our effort to draw closer to God after we realize how amazing He is. It is our way of acknowledging Him in every area of our lives.

As the Scripture says:

> *"Draw near to God and He will draw near to you. Cleanse your hands, you sinners; and purify your hearts, you double-minded."*
>
> James 4:8 NKJV

In this effort to get closer to God, the error comes when we try to package this experience in our own wrappings. The Scripture says it's God's gift. He can wrap His own presents. Just as no two marriages are identical and no two snowflakes are exactly alike, we all have slightly different journeys in Christ. Yes, there is only one way to God, but that does not mean everyone walking that way needs to buy identical hiking boots. The only constant and perfection in the experience is Jesus Himself, the Truth.

> Yes, there is only one way to God, but that does not mean everyone walking that way needs to buy identical hiking boots.

If you have a red pen (or whatever you value in your walk that isn't necessarily salvation based), I encourage you to keep doing what you are doing if it is working; however, demanding that others carry those "red pens" causes many to leave the church or refuse to come at all. Again, most of the world isn't rejecting Jesus, it is rejecting our presentation of Him.

Cutting Ham

My father told me an old story he had heard from another preacher. The story was about a family who had a tradition of cooking a delicious ham for the holidays. This family had a unique tradition of cutting the end of the ham off and then setting it to bake. Because of the success of the ham-baking experience, they continued this tradition from one generation to another. Until one day, a younger relative of the cook asked the cook why they always cut off the end of the ham. The cook didn't know so she went to ask her mother, who taught her how to bake the ham, why she had always cut the end of the ham off before baking. The mother casually answered, "So that it would fit in my pan because my pan was too small." Even though the next generation could have baked the whole ham in an appropriate-size pan, they continued cutting the ham because that was the way it had always been done and the ham was always tasty.

How much ham was wasted over the years simply because of the method the family associated with the preparation of the ham that had nothing to do with the flavor?

It is so important to understand what is essential to salvation and what are just add-ons done because the current times dictate their necessity. The Word of God and the Spirit of God is enough to lead and protect this generation of believers just as it has always been. There is no need to mandate any traditions as biblically necessary.

There is only one Truth that will always remain, Jesus Christ. The church will be in a better place and the Church Junkie can find healing when we stop using our red pens to mark the lives of other people.

> *"Do not take any of the things set apart for destruction, or you yourselves will be completely destroyed, and you will bring trouble on the camp of Israel."*
> Joshua 6:18 NLT

The above Scripture is taken from the book of Joshua. In this story, God gives Joshua instruction to bring the nation of Israel forward to take new territory. And in the conquering, they were *not* to claim anything that God intended for destruction. Some of the Israelites obeyed this instruction, while a few others took to their tents the things that God had warned against.

We see a few things in this story at once. One, God has things He will give us to keep and some other things that are meant to be eliminated. It's apparently very important to God that we don't get the two jumbled together.

Sometimes what God says doesn't always line up with what our past experiences or our logic tells us. Okay, make that most of the time. And sometimes, again most of the time, we are not comfortable with that. How much of church is just because we have always done it this way and how much of church is relatable and relevant to our current situation? I'm not talking about the message of the Bible. That is always relevant to the current culture. I'm talking about our methods of presenting the truths of the Bible. I'm talking about relevant messages and worship experiences, along with ministries that meet current needs.

Rarely will God's agenda fit our logic. God has always been willing to help the hurting and struggling if they are willing to give their lives to Him. I cringe at the idea that some of the worst sinners will be saved by the kind and generous grace of Jesus while long-time churchgoers may not make it into heaven's pearly gates.

> God has always been willing to help the hurting and struggling if they are willing to give their lives to Him.

The enemy shakes in terror when God's people enthusiastically obey Him. When God's people are unified in effort, there is nothing they cannot do as shown by the Tower of Babel. Do you know what the Tower of Babel represents? It represents people unified to such an extent that God said, "If as one people speaking the same language they have begun to do this, then, nothing they want to do will be impossible for them."

Genesis 11:6 ^NIV

What's wrong with that, one might ask. Well, they were united to carry out something that went against God's will. Just because something seems right to us, doesn't mean it's what God wants.

> *"There is a way that seems right to a man, but its end is the way to death."*
> Proverbs 14:12 ^ESV

"It just feels like church has become more focused on market surveys instead of moves of God to bring in souls. I don't want to be a part of that."

- Elijah

6
SHOWING UP IS HALF THE BATTLE

"And let us not neglect our meeting together, as some people do, but encourage one another, especially now that the day of his return is drawing near."
                              Hebrews 10:25 NLT

Small groups versus large gatherings? We see in Scripture where Jesus did both. And the larger a congregation gets the more vital it is to have both.

Because what people say they do and what they really do is often not the same thing, attempting to gather church attendance data is challenging at best. Also, for some, their weekly small group gathering is their "church attendance."

An article by Kelly Shattuck written for ChurchLeaders.com states:

Americans tend to over-report socially desirable behavior like voting and attending church and under-report socially undesirable behavior like drinking.

So, whereas a Gallup Poll puts church attendance at 40% it may be closer to 17%, writes Shattuck.[1]

And this same article states:

In another study surveying the growth of U.S. Protestants, Marler and Hadaway discovered that while the majority of Christians they interviewed don't belong to a local church, they still identify with their church roots.

And I have seen this to be true many times. People will say they are members of a church when, the fact is, that is in name only. They are not active participants of any church. But, I believe, *"they still identify with their church roots"* is a promise, God being true to His Word.

Proverbs 22:6 promises: *"Train up a child in the way he should go: and when he is old, he will not depart from it."* KJV

Many failed attempts at being a part of organized church attendance, I believe, consist of a mixture of bad experiences, laziness, misconceptions and "self-theology", which is when, based on our experiences, we have decided we know everything there is to know about God and we don't like Him, and He doesn't like us. But...Sometimes we need to forget what we think we know about God and start over.

> **Sometimes we need to forget what we think we know about God and start over.**

Because God does not just like us, He loves us. And He is in our corner. He would never have sacrificed His own son if He did not *know* there could be a perfect outcome for you and me.

I've heard it said that the hardest equipment to use at a gym is the front door. Maybe that truth could be said about the church as well.

I have a friend who shared with me a sad story. It was a story about his past family dysfunction. His mom and dad got a divorce when he was very young. His mom met a good man after the divorce and his dad remarried as well. Because of the divorce, he had to schedule when his father would pick him up to spend time with him. He said that he would dress in excitement and anticipation for that time he would be spending with his dad. His mom would help him pack his bags and he would wait in his room for his dad to come to get him. The problem was that his dad liked to party (one of the reasons for the divorce) more than he liked to spend time with his three children. So, his father would intend on picking up his kids, but would then be lured into having a good time (i.e. drinking and hanging out at a bar) so much so that he would forget or choose not to get his kids for the weekend. My friend said he would cry himself to sleep still hoping for his dad to just show up. His dad rarely did.

Grow Up and Show Up

The last thing you can tell an immature person is to "grow up." The only success to getting immaturity to go away is to give ourselves adequate motivation to change. As the old saying goes, "We will only truly change when the pain of staying the same is greater than the pain of change." In an all-out effort to get us to start showing up to church, let's dive into some of the reasons we are not showing up.

Reason 1: Change is Painful

Change is synonymous with pain. No one wants pain. We, by nature and self-preservation, avoid pain. Growing up is an intentional action that can sometimes be painful.

This is the lesson I learned from the birds.

The nest is a beautiful thing. We have some doves that frequent our house. They find a place to make a cozy nest to put their eggs. We go out of our way to allow this process to go as smoothly as possible.

One year the doves decided that a good place to make a nest was at the top of our back-porch light. This meant sneaking out our back door anytime we wanted to exit out through the back door of our house. Sometimes we forgot to carefully exit the back door and we would spook the momma bird.

The two young baby doves were growing but stayed in the nest with their mother. One day I forgot to sneak out the back door and came out like a bursting balloon. I slammed the door and spooked the two young doves, causing them to fly out of the nest. To my knowledge they had never ventured out of the nest before that day. It wasn't a beautiful flight, but they got the job done. I then realized that they could have flown out on their own but had decided that the familiar nest was more comfortable than taking a risk to fly like momma dove.

Showing up to church regardless of circumstances or conditions is a fantastic way to soar in your journey with God.

Reason 2: Time

> *Church attendance is an issue of priority not of time.* **What we do with our time is a direct reflection of our values.**

This may surprise some people, but I feel compelled to point out that everyone has the same amount of time each day. Yes, that's right; we all have twenty-four hours in a day and seven days in a week. *Church attendance is an issue of priority not of time.* What we do with our time is a direct reflection of our values. Spending time with God and His people is critical. I understand that maybe the church world has abused the idea of church by having too many gatherings and putting too much emphasis on one day of the week, but it still does not negate the biblical truth that God wants us to get together regularly.

I don't want to trivialize the importance and sometimes arduous endeavor of anyone who is trying to manage raising a family, work a demanding job, and juggle the many challenges of life. It is a topic that is worthy of discussion, though. God knew that the challenges of life would get harder and harder. He knew that as His return got closer, the temptations to drift would increase so He put a Scripture in Paul's heart that we were to be faithful to the gathering of believers. Isn't it interesting that more and more activities are being scheduled on the morning that most believers traditionally gather?

I believe the enemy of our soul is deliberately sabotaging our consistency. He is devaluing the gathering point or what we call church. His purpose is to disconnect us from our spiritual family. Like the baby water buffalo that has strayed from the herd with a hungry lion watching carefully, so is your enemy watching for the straying Christians who are drifting from the church.

Reason 3: Offense

It's just a matter of time. It happens to every believer who has ever lived. We will be tempted to be offended. We all can and do get our feelings hurt from time to time. It's part of walking side by side with humanity. Jesus Himself warned us that offenses are a natural part of life.

In his book *Unoffendable*, which by the way is a great read, Brant Hansen manages to say some fairly offendable things in a completely unoffendable way. You should read it. Or, if you are married to someone like my wife, you don't have to read it because you get it read to you, followed by a sermon. Pretty convicting.

Anyway, Hansen has a lot to say about this offended business; he wrote:

God is "allowed" anger, yes. And other things, too, that we're not, like, say—for starters—vengeance. That's His, and it makes sense, too, that we're not allowed vengeance. Here's one reason why: We stand as guilty as whoever is the target of our anger. But God? He doesn't...We can trust Him with anger. His character allows this. Ours doesn't.[2]

I think we tend to give our immoral behavior a free pass while holding others hostage for the same bad behavior.

> "Then said He unto His disciples, 'It is impossible but that offenses will come, but woe unto him through whom they come!'"
>
> Luke 17:1 KJ21

And He warned that He would take care of the offender. That means revenge is not our job. Revenge will never solve hurt feelings because pain cannot be transferred. It must be healed. What begins the healing process? Forgiveness. How can we forgive wrongs done us? By extending the mercy to others that was extended to us at the cross, that's how.

> **Revenge will never solve hurt feelings because pain cannot be transferred.**

Don't think you can? Then I recommend working on your generosity. God has some basics and one of them is you get what you give. In fact, He multiplies what you give…if your giving is sparse or mean spirited then that should scare you.

> "Give, and you will receive. Your gift will return to you in full—pressed down, shaken together to make room for more, running over, and poured into your lap. The measure you give will be the measure you get back."
>
> Luke 6:38 NLT

Let me tell you a story about the night Jesus quit.

My father was a pastor for nearly thirty years. In fact, I pastor the church that he once pastored. He was very innovative for his time. For about ten years we put on a massive production for Easter. It was the kind of thing that would draw thousands to our small church in rural Louisiana. We would practice for months for this one- or two-week event and it had a positive impact on our community. We would tell the story of Jesus through drama. It was an exceptional production. It was also a huge undertaking and needed a solid commitment for those making it happen. People would get tired and pleasant dispositions would get frayed.

One year right before the last practice was scheduled to begin for this life-changing event, someone tapped my dad on the shoulder and whispered, "Jesus just quit!"

I can't stop giggling at how this must have sounded to my father. What the whisperer was trying to convey was that the man playing the role of Jesus in our Easter drama had quit due to an offense. The drama was supposed to start the next day. Obviously, my dad had to do some damage control, but he was good at that and "Jesus" rejoined the team and Easter was a success.

This is one of the thousands, maybe millions, of examples of people getting offended in church. "Offenses will come," the Bible says. What do you do when your heart has been broken by the place that was supposed to bring healing?

> **What do you do when your heart has been broken by the place that was supposed to bring healing?**

It's not hard to understand that places that help us can

also hurt us, church being one of the best examples. But there is a significant difference between hurt and harm. The hurts God allows are not to harm us but to grow us.

Athletes get hurt all the time playing the sports they love. People get injured all the time working at the jobs that support their families. It is no huge wonder that church, as amazing as it can be, can also be a place that people get offended.

I like to ask people why they go to church. But I also like asking people why they don't go to church. The most common answer I hear is "too many hypocrites."

Funny thing about that is there are hypocrites at the grocery store too. Not only that but rude cashiers, outrageous prices, and our favorite ice cream sold out— so many things happen to us at the hands of those grocers who say we, the customers, are their number one priority. That doesn't stop us from getting groceries, though, does it? You ever thought about that?

We know we need food to live so we do what we must do to get that food. Not just for our sakes but our family must eat too. So, we get groceries. Every week. Sometimes, I feel like I see those people at the grocery store more than I see my mother. What we expect from the grocery store is for them to know their product and to deliver it. And we will take the good experiences, which are many, and the bad experiences, which are few, and just keep keeping on. I don't know about you, but I determine to be the pleasant person and present my best "me" regardless of the treatment I receive there because you never know what someone is going through and the kindness they receive from me may make all the difference in their day.

Want to know what I think we don't see? I think we don't see our need for God. We say we do. But our actions say we don't, not really. I think we don't see how fragile we are and how much better our life would be if it were centered on Him. And how when we see more clearly that makes it much easier for God to teach us how to allow others to be human and to make mistakes. After all, don't we want that same kind of consideration for our own failings?

Hypocrisy is defined as the practice of claiming to have moral standards or beliefs to which one's own behavior does not conform. After I examine myself, I find I can't find fault with another.

> *"Who are you to condemn someone else's servants? Their own master will judge whether they stand or fall. And with the Lord's help, they will stand and receive his approval."*
>
> Romans 14:4 NLT

I don't always behave as I should. Do you?

> **Our point of reference needs to be Jesus, not other people.**

Sometimes we need to see past ourselves, so we can see ourselves with the proper perspective. Our point of reference needs to be Jesus, not other people. Before Him we all fall short.

> *"Not that we dare to classify or compare ourselves with some of those who are commending themselves.* ***But when they***

> ***measure themselves by one another and compare themselves with one another, they are without understanding."***
> 2 Corinthians 10:12 ^{ESV}

John Bevere's book, *The Bait of Satan*, is a great read concerning our propensity to be offended. He wrote:

> *There is a false sense of self-protection in harboring an offense. It keeps you from seeing your own character flaws because the blame is deferred to another. You never have to face your role, your immaturity, or your sin because you see only the faults of the offender.*³

Look at this excerpt from Matthew that lets us know a few things about offense.

> "Don't judge others, or you will [so that you will not] be judged. You will be judged in the same way that you judge others, and ·the amount you give to others will be given to you [or the standard you use for others will be the standard used for you; ᴸ with the measure you measure, it will be measured to you]. Why do you notice the ·little piece of dust [speck; tiny splinter] in your ·friend's [ᴸ brother's (or sister's)] eye, but you don't ·notice [consider] the ·big piece of wood [log; plank; beam] in your own eye? How can you say to your ·friend [ᴸ brother], 'Let me take that ·little piece of dust [speck; splinter] out of your eye'? ·Look at yourself [ᵀ Behold]! You still have

> *that ·big piece of wood [log; plank; beam] in your own eye. You hypocrite! First, take the ·wood [log; plank; beam] out of your own eye. Then you will see clearly to take the ·dust [speck; splinter] out of your ·friend's [L brother's] eye."*
>
> Matthew 7:1-5 EXB

And the fact is that an offense never stays contained to the initial incident. That is what being unwilling to forgive does. It spreads throughout all our relationships until everything becomes an issue and we are left bitter and alone wondering why God has abandoned us.

Heavy stuff, I know. Maybe we should take a moment to reflect on how much we need Jesus.

Reason 4: Not Fitting In

Some people are just natural people magnets. My sister is one of them. Total strangers will see her at the local Walmart and tell her all about themselves. She has an empathic spirit that traps people in its orbit and they just gravitate closer. They feel safe with her. One of my assistants has been with my sister and watched her "work her magic" on other people. She said it was fascinating to watch in real time.

And then there are the rest of us…the ones who feel awkward and clumsy in situations where we might stand out. We don't know what to say, and when we do say something it comes out sounding weird and, well, awkward. And we may have had previous bad church experiences so there is that to contend with as well. Yes, let's take ourselves to c-h-u-r-c-h, that holy place that represents the presence of G-o-d so we can feel more awkward and out of place and weird. Who wants to sign up for that?? I'm slightly sick to my stomach just thinking about it.

But God wants that community of believers, that *ecclesia,* to happen. It's kind of a rock and hard place situation. Let me encourage you; do it anyway, regardless of how you feel. Keep searching until you find that place that you can call home.

Yes, it can be overwhelming. At our church we go out of our way to make everyone feel welcome, and that's why we also have community groups. A small group setting is perfect for people to get to know other people. That way, when in the larger service, they don't feel invisible and alone. Look for a church like that. Some place that is big AND small.

Get involved! I can't say that enough. Volunteering at your church is the best way to get to know other people and to grow in grace and in the knowledge of God.

Reason 5: Laziness

I would never put a paragraph about laziness in a book because I want to insult anyone. The reason I'm talking about it is because this is one of the reasons that participants in a survey gave as to why they don't go to church.

The only logic I have for this explanation is that we are overworked and, sometimes, over entertained. It has made us disciplined in making money, while lazy in the areas of spiritual discipline. Going to church is a lot like working out. We rarely feel like going until we get there but the results of the workout make us happy we went.

> "Diligent hands will rule, but laziness ends in forced labor."
>
> Proverbs 12:24 NIV

I believe this Scripture applies to secular jobs as well as in spiritual life. If you work hard and do things right, you will prosper on the job. If you work hard and are faithful to God and church, you will not end up a slave to sin.

Reason 6: Those people are out of touch

Once upon a time, there was a group of people who only did church one way and never changed it.

They are no longer a church.

The End

I know this must sound ridiculous and maybe even rude, but if we care about God's church and the way it functions, then we will feel the need to change our methods. We, the church, are taking a huge hit to our numbers because while there is an increase in progress in the world the church stays stuck in the past.

I confess that I love the fact that God doesn't change (Malachi 3:6) and that His Word lasts forever, but I don't think He meant that about what we do in our church services or worship experiences.

Look at this quote from an article on Crosswalk.com:

In the 1600s, sermons were regularly more than two hours long, and people were fined for falling asleep in church! Musical instruments such as the organ were considered worldly. Steeples or outdoor crosses on church buildings were looked down on as inappropriate. Aren't you glad that at least some of those ways of doing church have changed? [4]

Another word for change is growth. When we grow, we change. The church will always need growth. In other words, the church will constantly be changing. I think the problem is that we confuse method with message. The cornerstone of church should always remain Jesus Christ, He *is* the message. The method, however, to bring that message should be ever evolving. A church that stops changing will become focused on its own needs instead of the needs of others and the gospel message will take a back seat to personal comfort and individual desires.

> *"Do nothing from selfish ambition or conceit, but in humility count others more significant than yourselves."*
> Philippians 2:3 [ESV]

My family loves Disney. My wife and I save some money every couple of years and we go to good ol' Disney World. One of the rides that I make everyone go on every time we go is the Carousel of Progress. It teaches my children just how far we have come as a nation. The luxuries we enjoy now were not always available to us. It also gives them a picture of how things always change. You see, I want my kids to love change because I want them to love growing and getting better.

Progress usually comes at the price of comfort and the familiar. And that is the price we are often unwilling to pay. However, we also equally love the benefits of growth. So we usually find ourselves in a dilemma. Do we trade our comfort and certainty for progress or lose the potential of progress to keep comfort and familiarity? It sounds like a "no brainer" until you look at most religious institutions. Most denominations and churches across the world seem to be stuck in a time warp. They are standing for the right things but speaking in unfamiliar language.

Why would the church use concepts and methods those they are trying to reach cannot understand? Doing church with antiquated methods tells the outsider, "This church doesn't get me." When the outsider has no bridge to the church, the outsider stays on the outside. When the church understands that keeping up with the times is extremely important to reaching people with the Gospel, it will work on its bridges and outsiders can transition more easily to becoming insiders.

> **When the outsider has no bridge to the church, the outsider stays on the outside.**

Speaking the language of yesterday's church will give it an inside focus and make outsiders feel like the church is an exclusive club for perfect people and they aren't invited. When the casual Church Junkie gets immersed in the cause of following Jesus and leading others to the same experience, we will get on that Carousel of Progress and God can heal America.

The argument is usually made that the Scripture says not to be of the world, and rightly so. However, speaking in a way that the outsider understands does not make you worldly. It makes you a teacher.

Church Junkies across the world will have to make a choice of whether they want comfort from sameness or progress from obedience. I believe God is asking His church to love the lost more than we love the comforts of the way church has always been done. We have a commission to go into the world and teach the Gospel. I pray we speak their language and get our church experience on the Carousel of Progress.

"Thirty plus years of church involvement has proved to me that to be an active participant in church and never experience hurt is like believing you can work in a kitchen and never receive a burn while cooking. I am determined to never walk away from something that has helped me more than it has ever hurt me."

- Chermaine

7
IT'S NOT ALL ABOUT THE FEELS

We learn about God through the structure He calls the church. The word there is "ecclesia" or called-out ones. The church is made up of people who want to walk away from the life-corroding and destructive behaviors that we are all very familiar with in our world. These behaviors that cause so much pain to us all are called sin. Sin is disobedience to what God calls right or righteousness.

It is easy to look at a symptom and believe it to be the root cause. A runny nose is not the cause of a cold. It's a symptom. And it's not the symptom that causes the cold. The same holds true with the spirit man. The root is often hidden out of sight and must be dug up to truly be discovered. It is my belief that the real cause of crime, divorce, violence, addiction, depression, abuse, neglect, and all the other forms of human pain is the absence of God. You can't remove guns and resolve violence. You can't redefine marriage and stop divorce. You can't take a pill and solve depression. An addiction clinic will not end addiction. I'm all for treating these symptoms as needed, but to truly resolve these issues in our lives and hence our world, we need God.

We don't need to be seen, recognized, or noticed at nearly the capacity we think and pursue. Sometimes it's in the quiet service that we get the most lasting benefit. We may not recognize what brings lasting benefits because we use our feelings to gauge our health. But our feelings can be fickle and very unreliable. Maybe we need to stop asking ourselves how we feel and start asking ourselves what we know. Very rare is the Scripture that says, "this we feel" but there are plenty that say some variation of "this we know."

> **Maybe we need to stop asking ourselves how we feel and start asking ourselves what we know.**

God knows that our feelings will let us down, so He asks for commitment instead. He knows some days we just ain't gonna feel like being Christlike in attitude or actions. Lack of commitment has become so prevalent in our society, it must be taught. We have become so used to doing what we feel and getting out of something if it becomes difficult that we don't know what real commitment looks like.

Holiness, which is the nature of God, does not draw attention to itself one way or the other. I once heard a preacher say that no one was ever weirded into serving God. I agree with him. Just thought I'd throw that in as food for thought.

Weirdness is relative, by the way. Take Adam and Eve in the Garden of Eden for example. Eve never thought it was strange that a snake was talking to her. Hummm…I don't know about you, but I would have been *r-u-n-n-i-n-g* as fast as I could away from that weirdness. But, nope, not Eve. She carried on an entire convo with the scaly guy. And he convinced her to eat some fruit that her husband told her God said they were not to eat. This is the equivalent of, "Hey little girl. You want some candy?" What's up with that? Apparently conversing with reptiles was the norm back in the day.

What about God's plan? What is "normal" church? What does that look like in Scripture? Well the presence of God was there, and the truth of His Word was taught.

This means His message never changes.

What else? Oh, right, He left the method up to us.

"Growing up in church was scary and confusing, but also, something about it made me feel safe. I've learned the scary and confusing parts were man made, and the safety I felt was the love of my Heavenly Father."
- Jill

8
EXPOSE THE LIE, CATCH THE THIEF

God wants to bless you!
God wants to give me stuff?
Absolutely, yes.
What was your first thought? Was it all about your material needs being met? Be honest. This is not a test. If you answered yes, welcome to humanity. The part of us that lost connection with our Creator in the Garden of Eden is in a constant fight with the part of us that caused the lost connection.

Our heavenly Father loves us. There is nothing we can do or not do that will make Him love us any less than He loves us right now. Pretty much the most awesome news, right? And He desires to fill us with His love, His Spirit. A reconnection of what was disconnected by disobedience in the Garden.

Every worship gathering where the Holy Spirit is

present, and the Word of God is spoken, results in a blessing being poured out. Every time we are in the presence of God we are changed in some way. Empty vessels, hearts, are filled with godly desires when that blessing from God is received. The concept of being filled with God's Spirit is one that comes from His desire to bless us with all spiritual blessings.

> *"All praise to God, the Father of our Lord Jesus Christ, who has blessed us with every spiritual blessing in the heavenly realms because we are united with Christ."*
>
> Ephesians 1:3 NLT

Okay, so bring it, God. I'm ready.
Whoa! Pump the brakes a bit.
I think we need to talk about our responsibility first…

God's blessings come with an "If we do this, He'll do that" clause. But before you get too depressed about the concept, just know that He is on our side. He wants us to win. He is our champion. He doesn't break a contract.

So back to it.

The first order of this blessing business is to *receive* it. That might seem like a no brainer, but we all attend church or some type of community group looking for that missing piece to complete us. Some word of encouragement, some supernatural encounter with God, that missing piece.

We know we need something. And we find it. In Jesus. Yes? Absolutely yes! God desires to give us His blessings and if we receive them, those blessings will forever change our lives. This is the blessing we need for each situation in our lives. The foundation that will keep us steady. The connection that was denied us before we were born.

Yay and amen! So, I've fulfilled my end of the contract. Thanks, God, and see you later...

Whoops! Hold on, before you get carried away with this newfound grace, there is more.

What more? Why the challenge, of course. *What challenge?* There is always something or someone ready to sabotage the blessing. How do you protect the blessing you get from God, be it directly or through a church worship experience?

Before I answer that, we should know the enemies and the strategy employed to trick us.

The Beast Within

A benefit of spending time with my grandparents was watching movies. One of my favorite movies as a kid was *The Goonies*. In the movie, there was a sort of special guy who looked something like a monster. They called him Sloth. He liked Baby Ruth candy bars. Chunk was one of the kids who got caught by the bad guys and they put him in a room with Sloth. Sloth looked like something out of a horror movie and naturally, Chunk was scared out of his mind. The only thing Chunk knew to do was to feed Sloth. If he fed Sloth, Sloth would treat him like a friend. If he didn't, his life was in jeopardy.

We have this nature in us that the Bible calls Flesh. It is the ugly monster inside of us that has hunger rages. Flesh is most happy when you are feeding it but gets highly irritated when you don't. Flesh likes food like lust and pride plus an entire host of other harmful life foods.

Inside of us are two conditions fighting each other. One is the ugly monster called Flesh and the other is your spirit.

These next two sentences are important, so pay attention.

Flesh and Spirit have one thing in common. It is you.

Read the previous lines again. Let it sink in.

One hates what the other one loves and vice versa. Our flesh nature craves for the things that lead us away from God and our spirit man craves the things that lead us toward God. Whichever you feed, that is the nature that wins out and determines the quality of your spiritual life. Now we can infer that one of the main reasons we struggle spiritually, even though we are avid churchgoers, is because we feed the monster inside of us more than we feed the budding new life God gave us.

But we are not our only enemy.

The Evil One

Who's the sabotage crime boss of blessings? Satan. He once held a chief position in heaven. Until he didn't. His downfall was pride that elevated him to think himself equal with God.

In Luke 10:18 Jesus tells His disciples: *"'Yes,' he told them, 'I saw Satan fall from heaven like lightning!'"* NLT (If you need a point of reference, lightning travels from cloud-to-ground at roughly 200,000 miles per hour. No time to clear out his desk…just saying.) This is important to understand because if we think Satan has power equal to or greater than God, we will believe that Satan can wrest away from us that which God said is ours.

What does this mean in terms of Satan being your adversary? He is jealous of what was once his now being ours. He can't have it back, so he wants to make sure we either don't claim it, or if we do, we take no joy in it.

John 10:10 says: *"The thief's purpose is to steal and kill and destroy. My purpose is to give them a rich and satisfying life."* NLT

The thief Jesus is speaking of in John 10:10 is Satan. Now you know what he intends but it is just as important to recognize how he plans to do it.

Where's the leak?

Those who attend church receive something from God that makes us spiritually "rich and satisfied." We then leave to find an enemy whose sole aim is to steal, kill, and destroy everything that God has given us. And he doesn't always take it without our help; in fact, *he just needs to convince us that it is gone.* He steals the joy of having it by whispering that God is not faithful or forgiving or loving or kind toward us when we are faced with an unexpected hardship or an unkind word from a friend or an act of disobedience to God's Word.

We do the killing of the

> **We do the killing of the hope and we do the destroying of the connection we have established with God through our unbelief in the fidelity of God's promises to us.**

hope and we do the destroying of the connection we have established with God through our unbelief in the fidelity of God's promises to us.

It's rarely a quick process. Mostly, it's a slow leaching of all that is precious, like vital nutrients slowly being extracted from farming soil. Where are the blessings leaking out of your life?

Most of the time it can be traced back to the nature of the conversation between Eve and Satan in the Garden of Eden.

What?

Remember their conversation? Eve and the serpent? Genesis chapter 3 tells the story. CliffsNotes version: Satan had Eve questioning the goodness of God and His right to lay down some protective barriers.

> *"But who are you, a human being, to talk back to God? 'Shall what is formed say to the one who formed it, "Why did you make me like this?"'"*
>
> Romans 9:20^{NIV}

Wow! That's a strong verse, right? No one likes to be told what to do, but consider this analogy:

When a tire is flattening or there is an oil leak in the driveway, the leak must be found for the car to remain a safe means of transportation and for the tires and the engine to not be ruined. These are common sense solutions to protect what is valuable and precious. We don't view this maintenance as difficult or restrictive. We view it as protective and life giving.

> *"If you then, being evil, know how to give good gifts to your children, how much more will your Father who is in heaven give good things to those who ask Him!"*
>
> Matthew 7:11 NKJV

Thing is, there is a reason God doesn't always give us what *we* think is best for us. Eve took what she thought was best for her. It did not end well.

God isn't trying to ruin us but to reinstate us to His blessings, and once reinstated to reinforce the barriers between us and the thief so that nothing God has given us leaks out.

God supplied His Word to instruct us on how to protect ourselves from theft and if the robber does somehow sneak in during a "night season" God has provided His Spirit to sound the alarm.

Let's talk about sin. Get in your favorite lounging pajamas this could get a little uncomfortable.

Jeremiah was an Old Testament prophet. He is referred to as the weeping prophet. As we say in Louisiana, he passed some *misère, cher*.

> *"For my people have done two things: They have abandoned me—the fountain of living water. And they have dug for themselves cracked cisterns that can hold no water at all!"*
>
> Jeremiah 2:13 NLT

Bad thing #1 - They abandoned God.

Bad thing #2 - They dug their own blessing holder their own way.

God was frustrated with them because they turned from Him toward something else. Human reasoning, pop culture, social status…oh the things we run to as we abandon God. Building for ourselves what we think can hold a blessing but it's just a cracked cistern.

Let me get this straight. God's the living water, the blessing, and I have a cracked cistern… I think I'm seeing the problem here.

God is pouring Himself into us and we want it but can't keep it because our lives are lived in such a way that our blessing is leaking out.

Satan knows that when he can get us to sin, we are vulnerable to all of sin's destruction. God's living water, His blessing, has leaked out of our lives because guilt and shame have robbed us of our faith.

We often view God as the punisher, but the truth is God is the one that is giving us the opportunity to be healed of sin, to put our sin in remission. When He asks us to do something, it isn't to oppress us or to withhold good things from us. It is to protect and advance us.

When I hear someone say, "I feel so empty," I immediately think, "Seal the leak."

What should we do? It's a leak. Fix it. Too simple? No, this is exactly what God wants to do *for* us.

When Jesus died on the cross, He knew we could not fix ourselves. He fixed the sin leak for us. It's our responsibility to position ourselves to have that leak plugged and to be consistent with a lifestyle that keeps that leak permanently sealed.

Do you know what the word "repent" means?

Again, this is not a test. I think sometimes a churched brat like me can take for granted that people know things they don't know.

> Repent means to change one's mind. To turn around, go in a different direction.

Repent means to change one's mind. To turn around, go in a different direction. All God is looking for are people who want to live differently from the way they are currently living. People who want to receive the blessing, the grace that only comes from God.

When Jesus is the focus of your life, He will also be the fixer of your leaks.

I believe that the church is the mechanic shop in which Jesus is the chief mechanic. We can come with any depth of heartbreak, any seriously jacked-up life, or with seemingly no problems at all (yeah, you are lying about that last one) and He can fix it.

A true church specializes in making sure the "living water" is flowing and leaks are being sealed. Look for that in a church you want to call home; it is a sign of health.

"Church is a place where you will find both the realest and fakest people. I have been both. It's where I learned to lie, to others and to myself…but God. He is perfect and honest; never changing, never failing. Church is imperfect people pursuing a perfect God. There will always be hurt and brokenness amidst the joy and redemption."
- Bailey

9
WHAT'S NEXT?

Here we are, having explored all the challenges we face and the disappointing experiences we may have encountered, so what now?

Well, I think we need to begin again. Sometimes we need to forget what we think we know about God and start over. God is really big on the do-over. I am living proof of that.

I asked Siri what the opposite of benefit is, and it said, cost. For a moment my mind blanked and I couldn't take a full breath.

We have paid until we are bleeding sorrow, shame, and crushing disappointment. We have paid with the light of our souls until only darkness remains within. We have paid, and paid, and paid to live a life completely away from

> **We have paid until we are bleeding sorrow, shame, and crushing disappointment.**

God or worse we have paid, just as severely, by including God but using our own frame of reference to determine the rules by which salvation and deliverance come.

How foolish of us to not accept that the upfront cost is already paid, and the membership dues are so nominal and completely doable no matter our budget. Yes, there is a bit of sweat equity on our part, but the benefits far outweigh the labor.

Benefits Package

It is so easy to see the challenges of the church world without seeing the benefits. We hear what the media chooses to accentuate about the church. Our world loves to focus on pastors who make a lot of money or ministers who fall into eyebrow-raising sin. There is a real darkness that truly seeks to destroy the value of church in the minds of people. If the enemy of our souls can get us to disdain that which God ordained, then we won't experience the benefits of church.

The Biblical concept of church was meant to be a life-building movement. It was never meant to be a business or a negative experience. It is the life-giving movement that Christ had in mind when He came to save us. Once He saved us, He wanted us to work together to watch out for one another and to help those that have needs. The church is a safe place that we can go to get the equipping we need to please God in our everyday lives. It is the building mechanism that constructs the healthy networks of lifelong friendships and meaningful service.

Our children are our most precious possession. Even if you don't have children, you can probably still understand that statement. We seek to protect and provide for our children in every area. We want healthy food, behaving friends, safe places to learn and every other idea we can think of to help them.

The church is meant to be for children. God's children. Of which you are one. Jesus said that He wanted children to be allowed to come to Him.

> "Jesus said, 'Let the little children come to me, and do not hinder them, for the kingdom of heaven belongs to such as these.'"
>
> Matthew 19:14 NIV

Self-Feeders

We live in a fast-paced world. The idea of preparing a meal seems like a waste of time when you can just let someone else prepare it and all you must do is show up. The same trend and mindset seem to be in the church world. The church building becomes like a restaurant. You just show up and the musicians and singers have prepared worship, the preacher has prepared a spiritual meal and yes, we even have a kids' menu. None of that is bad or wrong and I believe in "showing up." I also believe that the one or two times we attend services or gatherings a week is not enough spiritual food to last you the entire week.

One of the key symptoms of a Church Junkie is the habit of only eating spiritual food when they are at the church building or watching it online. The fact is that the only believers who tend to stand the test of time and trials are the ones who learn how to be self-feeders. They are the ones who can take what they learn at church and apply it at home. They are the ones who have a personal daily prayer life. They are the ones who, in private, seek a relationship with God. They have a desire to know Him, not just know of Him. That determination cultivates within them a maturity that bleeds over into an unselfish desire to share what they know about God and to encourage others to grow a relationship with God.

The value of church and the online church community is real and recognized. If the choice is no church or online church, online church is the choice every time. I personally have watched our services online many times. Please don't feel as though I am against preparing a good service for the attendee or allowing a strong online viewing audience. I just simply believe that until we know how to seek God for ourselves, we will circle around the same issues in our lives without getting any real victory and progress.

Spiritual Meal Prep

When church is functioning at a Biblical level, the attendees understand that they have a personal responsibility not only for their own spiritual well-being but to some degree the well-being of others. We are to be meal preparers for our own spiritual eating needs and to be mindful of the spiritual hunger of others:

> *"Don't look out only for your own interests, but take an interest in others, too."*
> Philippians 2:4 NIV

It takes a personal relationship with Jesus and Holy Spirit power to cook up what our soul needs to be healthy.

Cooking only for taste is how we become unhealthy food addicts. Let's be honest, unhealthy food tastes the best. I have one cousin that has yet to allow her toddler to taste processed sugar. Why? Because she herself was addicted to it and knows that once he gets a taste of it he will no longer be satisfied with the sweetness of natural sugars. Healthy food can taste good, but it needs more cost investment, prep time and some taste bud adjustments. Spiritual growth is about feeding our inner man the righteousness of God, while training our destructive cravings to be in submission to us, not us to them.

Self-feeding is the essential key to unlocking the next chapter of the church. It will allow us to be stronger than the four walls we gather in and build healthy Christians instead of Church Junkies. The Church Junkie wants a fast food meal but a Mr. Universe body. One does not make the other.

> **The Church Junkie wants a fast food meal but a Mr. Universe body. One does not make the other.**

God is the ultimate cook; however, He seems to have a keen interest in our best efforts. He will help us in challenging times when we don't feel like we can feed ourselves. So, while I encourage you to become a self-feeder, I'm not suggesting that God won't take care of you. I'm saying that we have some responsibility in the matter. One of my favorite verses in Scripture is Psalm

23:5: *"Thou preparest a table before me in the presence of mine enemies: thou anointest my head with oil; my cup runneth over."* KJV

God can and will prepare our meals when the enemy of our soul comes to lay claim on our lives. God will provide because He is the ultimate provider, but that provision is for those that have done all that they can do.

> *"Therefore take up the whole armor of God, that you may be able to withstand in the evil day, and having done all, to stand firm."*
>
> Ephesians 6:13 ESV

I long for the day when members of God's church don't stumble into the building for the Sunday morning services like junkies needing a fix go stumbling to a drug dealer. I long for the day when we come to a Sunday, or whatever day of the week, service as a spiritually fit and healthy self-feeder ready to not only receive from God but to give a helping hand to those needing a leg up.

> *"But don't just listen to God's word. You must do what it says. Otherwise, you are only fooling yourselves."*
>
> James 1:22 NLT

The Plan

The Bible gives a model, a plan we should follow if we want to have a rich, successful life. Nothing in nature comes into being fully mature. Everything *grows* into maturity. We did not get like we are overnight, and we will not be different overnight. It's a process. Layers of the old are peeled away to reveal new and different layers underneath.

What does that plan look like, exactly? Remember the scripture reference from chapter one? It is Acts chapter 2, verse 42. This verse may be used as the perfect model for the process of attaining permanent change.

> *"They devoted themselves to the apostles' teaching and to the fellowship, to the breaking of bread and to prayer."* BSB

Let's break it down. According to this verse, the purposes/activities of the church should be **1)** teaching biblical doctrine, **2)** providing a place of fellowship for believers, **3)** observing the Lord's Supper, and **4)** praying.

Now let's explore these a bit. Why?

Because in these principles you will find the foundations that God intended for us to use in order for the gathering of the body of believers to have a positive effect in our life.

Teaching

If I ask one hundred people why they go to church I think I might get one hundred different answers. I wonder how many would say "to learn"? The teaching of Scripture is one of the core purposes of the church. Jesus wants you to be equipped for your life battles.

So, are you teachable? We bring with us our life experiences and we use those life experiences to interpret new life situations. It is far better to be open to the concept that you don't even know what you don't know about God than to fall into the unteachable trap of believing you know everything there is to know about God and His ways. Trust me when I say that if you know everything there is to know about God then He's not big enough to save either one of us.

Now, I'm not advocating we allow our common sense to leak out of our ears; instead ask God for guidance, read His Word and couple that reading and studying with the teaching from good solid leadership.

> *"Study to shew thyself approved unto God, a workman that needeth not to be ashamed, rightly dividing the word of truth."*
>
> 2 Timothy 2:15 KJV

> *"Give instruction to a wise man, and he will be still wiser; teach a righteous man, and he will increase in learning."*
>
> Proverbs 9:9 ESV

Friendship (a.k.a. Fellowship)

Another way to define fellowship is friends doing life together. Most of us don't expect friendships to be a major part of our spiritual growth, but biblically speaking, the human connection is a core asset to our church experience. Connecting to people that love Jesus is a critical part of our experience.

"Do not be ·fooled [deceived; misled]: "Bad ·friends [company] will ruin good ·habits [or character; morals; ᶜ a quote from the Greek poet Menander (c. 342-291 bc)]."

1 Corinthians 15:33 ᴱˣᴮ

"Two people are better off than one, for they can help each other succeed. If one person falls, the other can reach out and help. But someone who falls alone is in real trouble. Likewise, two people lying close together can keep each other warm. But how can one be warm alone? A person standing alone can be attacked and defeated, but two can stand back-to-back and conquer. Three are even better, for a triple-braided cord is not easily broken."

Ecclesiastes 4:9-12 ᴺᴸᵀ

"If anyone says, 'I love God,' and hates (works against) his [Christian] brother he is a liar; for the one who does not love his brother whom he has seen, cannot love God whom he has not seen."

1 John 4:20 ᴬᴹᴾ

Why do you hang around the people you hang around with? Similar interests? Both looking for the same things? Trust them to steer you in the right direction and give you a gentle brick to the head when you need it, right?

So, you get it then?

Need I say more…? I didn't think so.

Communion (a.k.a. the Lord's Supper)

Communion is the meal that heals! Whether the verse in Acts 2:42 is referring to the act of eating the wafer and drinking the grape juice or eating a meal with friends, its implication is the same: eating together while remembering what Jesus did for us is vital to the church. Hard to believe that something so simple would make it to central ideologies of the Bible, but it does.

> *"He took some bread and gave thanks to God for it. Then he broke it in pieces and gave it to the disciples, saying, "This is my body, which is given for you. Do this in remembrance of me."*
> Luke 22:19 NLT

> *"So Jesus told all the people to sit down on the ground. Then he took the seven loaves, thanked God for them, and broke them into pieces. He gave them to his disciples, who distributed the bread to the crowd."*
> Matthew 8:6 NLT

Breaking bread, though an uncommon term in modern culture, implies a letting down of our guard and sharing what we have with another. It requires trust and generosity of spirit and signifies being at peace with another.

Prayer

John Bunyan said, "We can do anything when we pray, but can do nothing until we pray." Prayer is the way we connect to God. It would seem silly to claim a connection to God without a prayer life. Prayer is the driving force of believers. It connects us to God and the destiny He has for us. A family that prays together stays together, and a church that prays together changes the world.

But what is prayer? The most basic definition of prayer is "talking to God." And by talking to God, I mean direct address to God. Just like if you and I were talking. It's verbal communication. And like all effective communication it requires listening, not just speaking.

> *"Do not be anxious about anything, but in every situation, by prayer and petition, with thanksgiving, present your requests to God. And the peace of God, which transcends all understanding, will guard your hearts and your minds in Christ Jesus."*
>
> Philippians 4:6-7 NIV

"The Sovereign LORD has given me his words of wisdom, so that I know how to comfort the weary. Morning by morning he wakens me and opens my understanding to his will."

Isaiah 50:4 NLT

> *"In the morning, O LORD, You hear my voice; at daybreak I lay my plea before You and wait in expectation."*
>
> Psalm 5:3 ᴮˢᴮ

Wait. Let me get this straight, I can talk to God about everything?

Yep.

But I thought He knows everything. Why do I have to tell Him?

We don't pray for God's benefit. We pray for our benefit. It relates faith and trust—ours to God. God is not looking for people that can right the mess they have made in their own life; He is looking for those willing to acknowledge that they are broken and trust Him to create something new and lasting in their life. And He does that when we trust Him enough to talk about it.

God is interested in us confessing what we did, not in why we did what we did. He already knows why.

> *"For the word of God is quick, and powerful, and sharper than any two-edged sword, piercing even to the dividing asunder of soul and spirit, and of the joints and marrow, and **is a discerner of the thoughts and intents of the heart**."*
>
> Hebrews 4:12 ᴷᴶⱽ

These simple mandates have a profound effect, a sort of spirit shock wave to those who practice them as a way of life.

Does this all seem too simple to be effective? Haven't we all been exposed to the complicated with little to no results? Religion is man's approach to God. And it has played out that we have created rituals and rules without impressive results. Let's instead seek God as His guidebook, the Bible, tells us. It is my belief that what you stand to gain by following the simplicity of the Gospel is far greater than anything you might chance to lose.

I'm rooting for you! And more importantly so is God. In fact, He is not only your supporter, He is your enabler. Trust Him to make what *He* wants happen for you.

Okay Church Junkie, are you ready?

Let's do this!

Together.

See ya' next Sunday!

ACKNOWLEDGMENTS

My Lord

"To God be the Glory" as the old song goes. God has been so good to me and I never want to stop thanking Him!

My Family

Thank you, my Keesha. Babe, you were the missing piece to all of my daydreams. Now that we dream together, life has taken a whole new meaning. I love you and know that this book wouldn't exist without your tireless support.

My Jensen and Miley, Dad loves you with all of his heart. You have always made be proud and I pray this book makes you proud. I love you. Jensen, you have always believed in dad and I believe in you. You can do anything God calls you to do. Miley, you will always be daddy's little girl and I can't wait to read the book you write.

My brother and sister, you rock! David, you are a leader and I am honored to call you my brother. Sarah, you have been a constant cheerleader regardless of how

I played the game of life. Both of you are a source of inspiration as we journey through this life together.

Dad and Mom, thank you for loving me unconditionally and 'training me in the direction I should go'. Dad, you have always made me believe I can do anything. This book is one of those "any things." Mom, you sacrificed so much so I could passionately live. I pray I'm "living" up to your expectations.

My Colleagues and Friends

Thank you to Chermaine Stein, known in our circles as Cher. You have made such an investment in our family and, for most of my life, have been helping me write. I would not have completed this book without you. God has given you a gift and you use it well.

Tony, Jill, Elijah, Bailey, Jeff, Judy and Shane, thank you for sharing a little bit of your church experiences and how it shaped your view of church.

Cannot let this book fly without thanking Scott and Leah Silverii. You both have a talent and passion for writing that inspires me. You were always willing to share your knowledge and insight. Thank you. And, then there is a shared love of ice cream…

Alli Worthington, no real words to express how thankful our entire team is for all you have done to move this process along. You are a blessing.

My House of Prayer church family I give thanks to you and for you. You have really supported me through this process and encouraged me through every step. Your generosity makes ministry fun and exciting.

NOTES

Chapter 2: Church Rehab

1. Kelly Shattuck, "7 Startling Facts: An Up Close Look at Church Attendance in America." *Outreach Magazine,* April 10, 2018,

https://churchleaders.com/pastor-articles/139575-7-starling-facts-an-up-close-look-at-church-attendance-in-america.html.

2. Dr. Tim Elmore, Generation iY: Secrets to Connecting with Today's Teens & Young Adults in the Digital Age (Atlanta, GA: Poet Gardener Publishing in association with Growing Leaders, Inc., 2015), 54

3. John Maxwell, "The Ten Commandments of Confrontation." *John C. Maxwell,* October 4, 2016, https://www.johnmaxwell.com/blog/the-ten-commandments-of-confrontation/.

4. Andy Stanley, *Deep & Wide* (Grand Rapids, MI: Zondervan, 2012), 54,68.

Chapter 3: More Than a Building

1. Emma Green, "It's Hard to Go to Church." *The Atlantic,* August 23, 2016,

https://theatlantic.com/politics/archive/2016/08/religious-participation-survey/496940/.

Chapter 4: The Sin Issue

1. Mathew Rodriguez, "Magic Johnson Wants You to Know He Isn't Cured of HIV He's Just Taking His Meds." TheBody, July 24, 2015,

www.thebody.com/content/76192/magic-johnson-wants-you-to-know-he-isnt-cured-of-h.html.

2. George P. Wood, "Redemption and Lift: Jesus changes both lives and circumstances." Influence Magazine, April 5, 2017,

https://influencemagazine.com/practice/redemption-and-lift.

3. Rodney Stark, America's Blessings: How Religion Benefits Everyone, Including Atheists (West Conshohocken, PA: Templeton Press, 2012), 4-5.

Chapter 6: Showing Up is Half the Battle

1. Shattuck, "7 Startling Facts: An Up Close Look at Church Attendance in America." *Outreach Magazine,* April 10, 2018.

2. Brant Hansen, *Unoffendable* (Nashville, TN: W Publsihing Group, an imprint of Thomas Nelson, 2015), 5.

3. John Bevere, *The Bait of Satan* (Lake Mary, FL: Charisma House, a part of Strang Communications Company, 1994/1997), 64.

4. Elmer L. Towns, Ed Stetzer, and Warren Bird, "The Church Changed, and Nobody Told Us." Adapted with permission from the authors from their book, Eleven Innovations in the Local Church, Regal, 2007, *Crosswalk*, January 1, 2008,

www.crosswalk.com/church/pastors-or-leadership/the-church-changed-and-nobody-told-us-11562925.html.

Made in the USA
Middletown, DE
24 August 2023

37284111R00078